The Gospel
according to
Angels

The Gospel according to Angels

Robert W. Graves

Chosen Books

A Division of Baker Book House Co.
Grand Rapids, Michigan 49516

Published by Chosen Books
a division of Baker Book House Company
P.O. Box 6287, Grand Rapids, MI 49516–6287

Printed in the United States of America

Library of Congress Cataloging-in-Publication Data

Graves, Robert W.
    The gospel according to angels / Robert W. Graves.
        p. cm.
    Includes bibliographical references and index.
    ISBN 0-8007-9263-7 (pbk.)
    1. Jesus Christ—Biography. 2. Jesus Christ—Teachings.
3. Angels. I. Title.
BT303.G68   1998
235'.3—dc21   98-25904

To my mother, Christine Hamrick Graves,
whose legacy to her children
is her tremendous trust
in the Word of God

"I have been sent to speak to you . . . to tell you this good news."

The angel Gabriel, recorded in Luke 1:19

Contents

Acknowledgments

I am indebted to a number of people for their contributions to the manuscript that became *The Gospel according to Angels*. A glance at the "Selected List of Works Consulted" in the back of the book will reveal some books that have shaped my thinking about the subject of angels. Although the Bible does not appear in this list, it has shaped my thinking more than all the others combined. You will not find any references in the list to the twentieth-century experiential genre of angel books or books that fall into the New Age category. I find these books too speculative, too anecdotal, too zany or too noxious to make trustworthy contributions to a reliable understanding of angels. If I were to allow them to shape a study of angels, I might as well throw in novels about angels, too. This would not do.

The following individuals were kind enough to critique the manuscript, in part or in whole: Dr. Charles Goodwin, president of Original Word Ministries; Dr. Stanley Horton, professor emeritus of the Assemblies of God Theological Seminary; Dr. Norman L. Geisler, dean of Southern Evangelical Seminary; Robert M. Bowman Jr., director of research, Atlanta Christian Apologetics Project; the Reverend Murray Tilles, director, Light of Messiah Ministries; and Emlie Carroll, Christian education instructor, Roswell (Ga.) Assembly of God Church. For their sacrifice of time, I am most grateful. Where I incorporated their suggestions, the book no doubt benefited; where I did not—well, time will tell. I would also like to thank Steve Gossett for his contribution to the alternate cover designs and Allen Brooks for the numerous times he has helped me with the computer.

Finally I would like to thank my editor, Jane Campbell, for her insightful comments that improved the book.

A View of God
from Another World

An Introduction

No one, we are told, has seen God in His infinite, awesome expanse and lived to tell about it (see Exodus 33:20). What a disappointment for us who long to see Him! There are no eyewitnesses to tell us about the very One who created us. No human eyewitnesses, that is. God created many creatures, and happily for us, one company of creatures is at least as intelligent and communicative as we are. These creatures, moreover, can look upon God and live to tell about it! I am, as you may have guessed, talking about angels.

Jesus tells us that angels dwell in the presence of God and gaze directly into the face of the Almighty. He said to His disciples, regarding a child in their midst, "See that you do not look down on one of these little ones. For I tell you that their angels in heaven always see the face of my Father in heaven" (Matthew 18:10). These guardian angels have a perpetual audience with the Father. So it would seem that angels communicate with God face to face. For those seeking eyewitness testimony about God, look no farther. We have it from the lips of Jesus—the angels know God in a personal way.

With authority Gabriel claimed, "I stand in the presence of God, and I have been sent to speak to you . . ." (Luke 1:19).

The apostle Paul attached distinct importance to the angelic eyewitnesses of the incarnate Christ:

> Beyond all question, the mystery of godliness is great:
> He [Jesus] appeared in a body,
>> was vindicated by the Spirit, was seen by angels. . . .
>
> 1 Timothy 3:16

Karl Barth, the twentieth century's preeminent theologian, who some say singlehandedly rescued the Word of God from nineteenth-century liberalism, wrote of angels:

> They are in the service of God. It is their existence and nature to observe the will of God and stand at His disposal. Their heavenly glory consists solely in this determination. . . . Moreover, they fulfil this service perfectly. They stand before the throne of God. They are at the place where the speech and action of God commence in the created world. They are its direct *entourage* and original witnesses.[1]

The fact that angels are eyewitnesses of God and witnesses of the incarnation of the Son of God is necessary to qualify them as witnesses, but it is only half the test. A witness must also be credible, his integrity unquestioned, his character sterling. For this reason we must also examine the character and nature of angels.

Jesus calls those angels "holy" with whom He will return to earth (Mark 8:38; Luke 9:26). The apostle John tells us that the angels overseeing the judgment of those who receive the mark of the Beast are also "holy" (Revelation 14:10). A certain angel is described as coming down from heaven with great authority, "and the earth was illuminated by his splendor" (Revelation 18:1).

Angels are also powerful. When the Lord Jesus is revealed from heaven, He will come "in blazing fire with his powerful angels" (2 Thessalonians 1:7).

Furthermore, angels are cautious about what they say, taking care not just to speak the truth, but to measure their words lest they overstep their authority. The apostle Peter tells us that there are arrogant men not afraid to slander fallen angels, whereas "even [the holy] angels, although they are stronger and more powerful, do not bring slanderous accusations against such beings in the presence of the Lord" (2 Peter 2:11). Unlike Satan, whom Jesus describes as "the father of lies" who, when he does lie, "speaks his native language" (John 8:44), the "native language" of the holy angels is truth.

Barth called the angels "infallible witnesses":[2]

> . . . God's pure witnesses, beside whom there is none to compare on earth, who are therefore needed on earth, and who by the goodness of God are given to us in their reality. They are pure witnesses because they are heavenly beings. They are heaven itself coming with God to earth and invading the earthly world.[3]

Angels are confident about the truth of their message. The priest Zechariah discovered that expressing doubt to an angel concerning his message can be dangerous to your health! He was temporarily stricken mute (and perhaps deaf) for his brash skepticism (see Luke 1:5–25, 57–64).

One last question needs to be answered: Are angels communicative? We know that intellectually they are superior to humans, whose condition has been described as "a little lower than the angels" (Hebrews 2:7). Also, angels are curious. The apostle Peter describes them as longing "to look into" the ways of the Lord relating to the salvation of the human race (1 Peter 1:12). But are they communicative?

The linguistic history of the very word *angel* answers the question. In Hebrew and Greek, the languages of the Old and New Testaments, the word for "angel" means *messenger*. St. Augustine stated it forthrightly: "It is not because they are Angels that they are Angels. They are Angels because they are sent, for the name *Angel* refers to their office not to their nature."[4] It is the nature of angels to "do [God's] bidding" (Psalm 103:20); and communicating God's message to man is one duty in their job description. Look at the unusual concluding statement of the angel at the vacated tomb of Jesus. After bearing witness to Jesus' resurrection, he says, "Now I have told you" (Matthew 28:7), as though he were saying, "For this purpose I was sent to you. My task is fulfilled."

In *What the Bible Says about Angels,* one of the more biblical works on angels, Dr. David Jeremiah writes the following concerning the Hebrew and Greek words translated *angel:*

> The core meaning of both those words is *messenger.* That's the essence of who and what angels are. They are couriers for Someone other than themselves. They're Someone else's ambassadors, Someone else's agents. They represent only him, and never themselves. They are channels to carry only his information. They speak and act according to his instructions and they bear his authority.
>
> . . . Apart from God, angels can do nothing and are nothing. Their very food and drink is to do his will and accomplish his work. And God's will and work for angels is to *communicate his messages,* both by what they say and what they do.[5]

Are angels conversant? An angel tells the prophet Zechariah, "I will show you . . ." (Zechariah 1:9). Another angel tells John, "I will explain to you the mystery . . ." (Revelation 17:7). Certainly angels are intelligent, communicative beings.

Furthermore the Scriptures make it clear that God trusts His holy angels to deliver His messages. God reveals to John in a vision an "angel flying in midair, and he had the eternal gospel to proclaim to those who live on the earth—to every nation, tribe, language and people" (Revelation 14:6). Jesus Himself says to John, "I . . . have sent my angel to give you this testimony" (Revelation 22:16). According to J. R. Edwards, angels "appear as . . . proclaimers of news or mediators of revelations from God."[6] We can be sure that the holy angels of God are dependable couriers, delivering their messages just as they are given them.

Given the evidence of their trustworthiness, it would be an insult to suggest that angels be sworn in before giving testimony! However, one angel was:

> Then the angel I had seen standing on the sea and on the land raised his right hand to heaven. And he swore by him who lives for ever and ever, who created the heavens and all that is in them, the earth and all that is in it, and the sea and all that is in it. . . .
>
> Revelation 10:5–6

You will discover what he swore to in the pages that follow.

Given the nature of angels and their appearances at pivotal junctures in the history of the redemption of the human race (notice how they punctuate the life of Jesus: conception, birth, resurrection, ascension and Second Coming), it is little wonder we become infatuated with angels! Unfortunately this often blinds us to the actual words these messengers were sent to deliver. The mistake we humans make is illustrated fittingly by Edwards:

The fascination with angels in themselves rather than with the purpose for which they are sent is not unlike the misperception on the part of a dog that looks to the pointed finger rather than the object pointed to.[7]

Along these lines but from the perspective of angels, Barth writes:

> They always look away from themselves, and they invite and command others to look away from every creature, themselves included, to the One who alone is worthy that the eye of every creature should rest on Him.[8]

Instead of putting angels under microscopes, we should put them in front of microphones. For they have seen God, and more importantly, God has spoken to them words meant for human ears. For this reason, in the pages that follow, I have slipped a microphone in front of the angels of God. Let those who have ears hear, for the angels do not speak their own words, but the very words of God.

The Apostles' Creed

A creed is a confession of faith or brief statement of beliefs, from the Latin *credo*, "I believe." The Apostles' Creed is one of the earliest creeds of Christianity. Because of the delicate nature and thus the scarcity of ancient written documents, it is difficult to determine with precision the date of origin of the Creed. We have copies of it, in a briefer form, dating back to A.D. 340, and a baptismal catechism of it dating back to the second century A.D. Because the teachings of the Creed comport in detail with the apostolic teachings of the New Testament, it is safe to say that the Creed was inspired by either the oral or written teachings of the apostles.

The Apostles' Creed distills the Christian faith into three primary statements and nine secondary statements—four that describe Jesus and five that relate to believers:

I believe in God the Father Almighty, maker of heaven and earth;
and
In Jesus Christ, His only Son, our Lord;
> *Who was conceived by the Holy Spirit, born of the Virgin Mary;*
> *Suffered under Pontius Pilate, was crucified, dead and buried;[9]*
> *the third day He rose from the dead;*
> *He ascended into heaven and sits at the right hand of God the Father Almighty;*
> *From thence He shall come to judge the living and the dead;*
and
I believe in the Holy Spirit;
> *The holy catholic Church;*
> *The communion of the saints;*
> *The forgiveness of sins;*
> *The resurrection of the body; and*
> *The life everlasting. Amen.*

Taken together, these twelve statements may be considered the essential tenets of Christianity. The beliefs are so basic that someone has said they are common to every denomination of Christendom. (No small feat, since there are more than two hundred denominations in the United States alone!) Textual criticism and paleographic research have confirmed the pristine and nascent character of the creedal statements. And, as we shall see, the angels themselves add their voices in proclaiming the truth of each significant statement within the Creed. Although the origins of these beliefs can be traced back to the very beginning of Christianity, neither time nor heretic has succeeded in corrupting them; neither tyrant nor philosopher in eradicating them.

There is no reason to believe that those who formulated the Apostles' Creed had angelic utterances in mind or were inspired by such declarations. After all, it is the Apostles' Creed, not the Angels' Creed. Yet as the course of providence would have it, every primary component of the Creed receives angelic attestation. It would seem that the apostles indeed listened carefully to the message of those who came from before the face of God.

Because the nature of the Creed is to encapsulate the central beliefs of the Christian faith, and because certain chapters in this book are devoted to those beliefs, I have inserted an Apostles' Creed sidebar into relevant chapters.

Part 1

King of Kings and Lord of Lords

What Angels Believe about Jesus

The life of Jesus is framed by angelic activity. In fact, five hundred years before His birth, an angel revealed His coming; and at His Second Coming, a host of angels will accompany Him as He returns to earth. Between these events, from conception to ascension, His life was punctuated by angelic appearances.

The angels spoke to Mary and Joseph during Jesus' infancy, and even before. Angels announced His birth to shepherds in the fields. Angels ministered to Jesus during His desert experience and in the Garden of Gethsemane just before His arrest. They appeared at His empty tomb after His resurrection. One rolled back the stone from the front of the tomb. It is not too farfetched to believe that angels were at His side as He arose from the dead. Finally two angels appeared as He ascended into heaven.

Interestingly, though, the ministry of angels as messengers seemed to cease during the ministry of Jesus. And why shouldn't it? The Word had come to earth.

In the gospels and Revelation, Jesus referred to angels 32 times. He knew them well and described them in some detail, revealing things never before divulged. But more to the point, certain angels have unveiled truths about Jesus.

In this section we find out exactly what the angels knew and revealed about the Son of God.

1

Jesus: Conceived by the Holy Spirit, Born of a Virgin

An angel of the Lord appeared to him in a dream and said, "Joseph son of David, do not be afraid to take Mary home as your wife, because what is conceived in her is from the Holy Spirit."

Matthew 1:20

It is apparent from what the angelic messenger said that angels are very aware of human experience, including emotions. For Mary, an unmarried woman, to have become pregnant would have been scandalous! Thus the angel assures her betrothed, Joseph, that Mary has not been unfaithful to him. Indeed, in the following dialogue between the angel and Mary, taken from Luke 1:30–35, the angel implies that Mary is a virgin:

Angel: "Do not be afraid, Mary, you have found favor with God. You will be with child and give birth to a son. . . ."
Mary: "How will this be, since I am a virgin?"

21

Angel: "The Holy Spirit will come upon you, and the power of the Most High will overshadow you."

But God's choosing a virgin, though important, is not the major emphasis of the angel's message to Mary. More vital is that Mary conceived Jesus by a supernatural act of God the Father, which has certain implications about the exclusiveness and validity of Christianity.

For this can be said of no one else in history. No Old Testament figure was conceived like this. Neither Buddha nor Mohammed was conceived by the Holy Spirit (although, interestingly, Islam does teach that Jesus was born of a virgin). The conception of only one other figure even approaches this kind of supernatural act of creation: Adam, the first human who ever existed. His uniqueness is of a different category, however, than that of Jesus. So distinct are the two that the apostle Paul describes them like this: "The first man was of the dust of the earth, the second man from heaven" (1 Corinthians 15:47).

Jesus exclusively was begotten in the fashion the angel recounts. If so, this validates every word He spoke, whether about His Father, Himself, the Holy Spirit or human sin and forgiveness. The uniqueness of Jesus' conception certifies the veracity of His teachings.

The words of the angel to Joseph on that memorable Palestine night are clear and beyond misunderstanding: Jesus was born of a virgin, who conceived Him by a supernatural act of the Holy Spirit.

"Who was conceived by the Holy Spirit, born of the Virgin Mary"

In the gospels of Matthew and Luke, an angel names Mary as the woman who will give birth to the Son of God. After Mary conceives Jesus, an unnamed angel tells Mary's betrothed, Joseph, planning in pain and perplexity to break his engagement with Mary due to her pregnancy, not to fear but to "take Mary home as your wife, because what is conceived in her is from the Holy Spirit" (Matthew 1:20).

In the gospel of Luke, the angel Gabriel, speaking directly to Mary, startles her with, "Greetings, you who are highly favored! The Lord is with you" (1:28). Sensing her fear, Gabriel tries to comfort her: "Do not be afraid, Mary, you have found favor with God. You will be with child and give birth to a son, and you are to give him the name Jesus" (Luke 1:30–31). Mary rightly asks, "How will this be since I am a virgin?" (verse 34).

Tacitly accepting the assertion of Mary's virginity, the angel explains how it can be that she, never having been with a man, will become pregnant: "The Holy Spirit will come upon you, and the power of the Most High will overshadow you. So the holy one to be born will be called the Son of God" (verse 35).

2

Jesus: Named by an Angel

On the eighth day, when it was time to circumcise him,
he was named Jesus, the name the angel had given him
before he had been conceived.

Luke 2:21

Normally a child is named by his or her mother or father,
or perhaps a grandparent, uncle or aunt. Interestingly, this
child, whom "God exalted . . . to the highest place and
gave . . . the name that is above every name, that at the
name of Jesus every knee should bow, in heaven and on
earth and under the earth, and every tongue confess that
Jesus Christ is Lord, to the glory of God the Father" (Philippians 2:9–11), was named by an angel. As John Calvin
wrote, "The name 'Jesus' was bestowed upon him not
without reason or by chance, or by the decision of men,
but it was brought from heaven by an angel. . . ."[10]

The angel who visited Joseph told him, "[Mary] will
give birth to a son, and you are to give him the name
Jesus . . ." (Matthew 1:21). In Luke we learn the identity

of the angel who named Jesus; it was Gabriel (1:26). He said to Mary, "You will be with child and give birth to a son, and you are to give him the name Jesus" (1:31).

Gabriel, as a messenger of God, was simply delivering the mind of God to human minds. Nevertheless, the name given the Savior of this fallen world rolled first from the lips of an angel. What a privilege for Gabriel to be chosen as the first being to vocalize to Adam's race the name of earth's Redeemer!

And how appropriate that His name be *Jesus* (or *Y'shua*), for it means in Hebrew "The Lord saves."

The Messiah, Jesus, would be known by many names and titles—everything from "Alpha" to "Omega," "the First and the Last, the Beginning and the End" (Revelation 22:13). He would be called "the Almighty," "the Most Holy," "Wonderful Counselor," "Prince of Peace," "the Word of life," "the Word of God" (Revelation 1:8; Daniel 9:24; Isaiah 9:6; 1 John 1:1; Revelation 19:13). He would reveal Himself as the great "I am" (John 8:58). He would be given many more names and titles—but none so precious as that planted in the heart of Mary by the angel Gabriel: *Jesus.*

In the 1970s I served on the board of deacons at a church in Marietta, Georgia, with a Christian gentleman who learned in an unusual way the preciousness of the name of Jesus. He and his wife suffered the horrible pain of being told by their doctor that their newborn daughter had been injured during delivery and would never live more than a vegetative life. She would never walk, talk, write or play. The parents spent the months that followed praying over their baby girl in the name of Jesus, pleading Jesus' name over their darling daughter.

One day, after many months of prayer, the mother thought she heard her daughter say something. She listened closely. The tiny girl was speaking a word! It was the name she had heard her mother utter so frequently above her crib: *Jesus.*

This little girl went on to graduate from high school and attend classes at Louisiana State University. But even these achievements are overshadowed by the depth of her spiritual acumen and sensitivity.

This is only one of many stories that illustrate why, of all of the names and titles of the Messiah, *Jesus* is the most precious.

3

Jesus: Worshiped by Angels

Then I looked and heard the voice of many angels, numbering thousands upon thousands, and ten thousand times ten thousand. They encircled the throne and the living creatures and the elders. In a loud voice they sang: "Worthy is the Lamb, who was slain, to receive power and wealth and wisdom and strength and honor and glory and praise!" Then I heard every creature in heaven and on earth and under the earth and on the sea, and all that is in them, singing: "To him who sits on the throne and to the Lamb be praise and honor and glory and power, for ever and ever!" The four living creatures said, "Amen," and the elders fell down and worshiped.

Revelation 5:11–14

This passage from Revelation is reminiscent of Isaiah's vision of seraphim (or seraphs) in worship of God (6:1–4). There are no greater descriptions of praise in all the Bible than these passages filled with wonder, mystery and awe— heavenly creatures never again mentioned in the Scriptures, hovering around the Lord on His throne and calling to one another, "Holy, holy, holy is the Lord Almighty. . . .' At the sound of their voices the doorposts and thresholds shook and the temple was filled with smoke" (verses 3–4).

According to Ron Rhodes in *Angels among Us:*

> . . . What Isaiah actually saw was Jesus' glory (John 12:41). The words of Isaiah 6:3 refer to the glory of "the Lord Almighty" (or, more literally, the *Yahweh of hosts),* but John says these words were actually in reference to Jesus Christ. Jesus and Yahweh are here equated.
>
> How awesome this must have been for Isaiah! About 700 years before the Messiah was born in Bethlehem, Isaiah saw the glory of the preincarnate Christ in a vision. And the One whom Isaiah had personally encountered in this vision is the same One whose birth he prophesied. . . . The One Isaiah beheld in this vision—worshiped by the holy angels—is the same One who would be served by those same angels when He became a human being in Bethlehem.[11]

John seems to be describing the same throne in Revelation 5, only now it is at the culmination of history, with time swallowed up in eternity. All of creation is singing praise to God, including myriad upon myriad of angels (see verse 11).

If we know anything about angels, it is this: They know that God alone is worthy of worship. (More on this in chapters 20, 21 and 22.) How is it, then, that innumerable angels are described here as worshiping Jesus? And what does this worship of Jesus imply?

Only one answer satisfies the facts: The One we know as the Son of God is God the Son. Unless the Lamb is God, there is no justification for the angels to worship at the feet of the Lamb.

Who is the "Lamb"? John the Baptist tells us: "The next day John saw Jesus coming toward him and said, 'Look,

the Lamb of God, who takes away the sin of the world!'"
(John 1:29). The reference is to the Old Testament prac-
tice of sacrificing to God a perfect lamb on the altar for the
sins of the people (see Exodus 12). Jesus served as the
Lamb once for all (see 1 Peter 1:18–21; Hebrews 7:27; 9:12,
26; 10:10–14).

Why is this Lamb worthy of worship? If the nature of
God is triune, the question is answered. If this is not your
conclusion, you must explain why angels, who worship
God alone, worship Jesus.

4

Jesus: Exclusively Worthy

> I saw a mighty angel proclaiming in a loud voice, "Who is worthy to break the seals and open the scroll?" But no one in heaven or on earth or under the earth could open the scroll or even look inside it. I wept and wept because no one was found who was worthy to open the scroll or look inside. Then one of the elders said to me, "Do not weep! See, the Lion of the tribe of Judah, the Root of David, has triumphed. He is able to open the scroll and its seven seals."

> Revelation 5:2–5

This is an incredibly meaningful passage of Scripture. But because it is filled with symbolism and allusions, its significance escapes many.

First, note that John is in heaven (4:1–2). The throne John sees is in heaven, too (4:2). Next, notice that whoever is sitting on that throne is worshiped by the surrounding elders ("an exalted angelic order," according to Mounce, pp. 135–36) and creatures with praise of, in Judith Lang's words, the "highest created voice":[12]

"Holy, holy, holy is the Lord God Almighty, who was, and is, and is to come. . . . You are worthy, our Lord and God, to receive glory and honor and power, for you created all things, and by your will they were created and have their being."

Revelation 4:8, 11

Sitting on this throne in heaven, then, is almighty God.

An angel asks, "Who is worthy to break the seals and open the scroll?" The scroll contains God's plan for the universe, including the consummation of fallen humanity—one branch (the redeemed) finding its cure in the redemptive work of Christ, another branch (the unrepentant) finding its cure in another aspect of the love of God—a love so powerful and pure that it negates the unloving.

Only if the seals can be broken and the scroll opened will evil be terminated, unfolding, as it were, to reveal the beauty of God's nature—His grace, mercy, love and holiness. But none is found worthy to open the seal—no one on the earth; no one under the earth; no one even in heaven!

What about God the Father? He was in heaven. Why was He not considered worthy to open the scroll? Would this not be an affront to the Almighty? Not according to Karl Barth, who in his discussion of the sharing of the heavenly throne found the answer in the triune nature of the Godhead:

[The] Father can as little be limited, rivalled or even effaced by the Son as He for His part can limit, rival or efface the Son. It is only when the Son works that He really works. They are not two persons in our sense of the term, i.e., two different subjects which will and work independently, so that their activities might cut across and restrict one another, and necessarily give rise to a conflict of priority and authority. But as the ancient doctrine of the Trinity had it, they are two modes of being . . . of the one divine Subject, two times the one God, the one omnipotent will, the one eternal righteousness, goodness and mercy.[13]

We see in Revelation 5:5 that "the Lion of the tribe of Judah, the Root of David, has triumphed. He is able to open the scroll. . . ." At this time the elders and creatures surrounding the throne sing a new song. This is when we discover why only the Lamb is worthy to open the scroll:

> And they sang a new song: "You are worthy to take the scroll and to open its seals, because you were slain, and with your blood you purchased men for God from every tribe and language and people and nation."
>
> Revelation 5:9

The names *Lion of the tribe of Judah, the Root of David* and *the Lamb* all refer to Jesus, the *Logos* (Greek for *Word;* see John 1:1) incarnate. Only the Son is worthy to open the seal because only He executed an act of total self-sacrifice. God the Father was not slain for the sins of humankind; God the Son was. The apostle Paul confirmed this when he told the Christian leaders from Ephesus, "Be shepherds of the church of God, which he bought with his own blood" (Acts 20:28).

The God who is Creator of all, who formed a creature with a will free to choose, free to worship or rebel, free to love or hate, did not isolate Himself from His creation. Unlike the gods of others that insulate themselves from the creation, from its pain and curses, from its violence and death, Jesus, "being in very nature God . . . made himself nothing . . . being made in human likeness . . . and became obedient to death—even death on a cross!" (Philippians 2:6–8). This is why the Son of God is exclusively worthy to open the scroll.

The scroll reveals a time of judgment and pain across the earth. And lest man cry foul to a god buffered from pain and suffering, the triune Godhead willed to know, through the person of the Son, rejection, sorrow, pain and suffering, even at the hands of His beloved creation, so that His creatures might be reconciled to Him and know Him gloriously face to face.

Robert Mounce, in his respected commentary on Revelation, states it like this:

> The Lamb is worthy to open the book for a threefold reason: he was slain (a historical fact), he purchased men unto God (the interpretation of that fact), and he made them a kingdom and priests (the result of the fact). That the same ascription of worth is directed both to the One upon the throne (4:11) and to the Lamb (5:9) indicates the exalted Christology of the Apocalypse.
>
> The worthiness of the Lamb does not at this point stem from his essential being, but from his great act of redemption. He is worthy precisely because he was slain. His sacrificial death was the means whereby he purchased men unto God.[14]

5

Jesus: King of Kings and Lord of Lords

"He will be great and will be called the Son of the Most High. The Lord God will give him the throne of his father David, and he will reign over the house of Jacob forever; his kingdom will never end."

Luke 1:32–33

Then I heard every creature in heaven and on earth and under the earth and on the sea, and all that is in them, singing: "To him who sits on the throne and to the Lamb be praise and honor and glory and power, for ever and ever!"

Revelation 5:13

From Jesus' conception to His heavenly coronation, the angels confirm that His reign will be eternal. Gabriel states it in the negative: "His kingdom will never end" (Luke 1:33). Millions upon millions of angels and other creations of God state it in the positive: "To him who sits on the throne and to the Lamb be praise and honor and glory and power, for ever and ever!" (Revelation 5:13).

There is no room left for other human-imagined gods, neither in time nor in space, for geographically the heavenly creatures around the throne of God have told us that Jesus' blood "purchased men for God from every tribe and language and people and nation" (Revelation 5:9). The power in the blood of Christ transcends time and space. It was efficacious for a first-century Palestinian and it will be efficacious for a twenty-first-century American.

The power and penalty of sin were broken once and for all in the one visitation and sacrifice of the eternal Son of God. He need not come a thousand times to a thousand tribes:

> Christ did not enter a man-made sanctuary that was only a copy of the true one; he entered heaven itself, now to appear for us in God's presence. Nor did he enter heaven to offer himself again and again, the way the high priest enters the Most Holy Place every year with blood that is not his own. Then Christ would have had to suffer many times since the creation of the world. But now he has appeared once for all at the end of the ages to do away with sin by the sacrifice of himself.
>
> Hebrews 9:24–26

Jesus was not merely one of many kings or one of many lords. These titles mean that all the kings of the earth are ruled by one heavenly King: Jesus. All the lords of the earth are ruled by one heavenly Lord: Jesus.

> "They will make war against the Lamb, but the Lamb will overcome them because he is Lord of lords and King of kings. . . ."
>
> Revelation 17:14

After all, given the nature of the Son of God—"In the beginning was the Word, and the Word was with God, and the Word was God. . . . The Word became flesh and made his dwelling among us. We have seen his glory, the glory of the one and only, who came from the Father, full of grace and truth" (John 1:1, 14)—it is ludicrous to suggest that there could be a king or lord over Him! That is tantamount to suggesting that there could be a God over God.

Jesus alone is King of kings and Lord of lords.

6

Jesus: Savior of Humankind

"She will give birth to a son, and you are to give him the name Jesus, because he will save his people from their sins."

Matthew 1:21

"Today in the town of David [Bethlehem] a Savior has been born to you; he is Christ the Lord."

Luke 2:11

The angel's announcement to the shepherds that night was not merely that "a Savior has been born to you" (Luke 2:11), although that in itself would have been truly good news. But the angel made it clear he was not talking about a political savior who had come to deliver his people from the bondage of Caesar. Rather, this Savior had come to deliver his people from their sins.

To save from sin is, of course, on a plane far above mere salvation from political bondage. Several historical figures have achieved the latter, but no human being has ever

37

presumed to save people from spiritual bondage or the penalty of sin. Such a metaphysical feat is beyond the ability of any human. Only God can forgive sins—which is why many of Jesus' contemporaries accused Him of blasphemy and tried to execute Him on the spot when He forgave sins (see Matthew 9:1–8; Mark 2:1–12; Luke 7:44–50).

For the descendants of Abraham, and for every tribe and culture that understands the spiritual imperfection and wickedness of human nature, the arrival of the Savior was indeed, as the angel said, "good news of great joy that will be for all the people" (Luke 2:10). On that Bethlehem night, the refrain of praise that burst forth from the great company of heavenly angels drew the Savior's line of descent from heaven to earth, leaving no doubt about where the Savior was from and to whom He was sent: "Glory to God in the highest, and on earth peace, good will toward men" Luke 2:14 (KJV).

For millennia a sense of right and wrong had permeated all tribes and peoples on the face of the earth, and a need to make offering and sacrifice to God or gods was sensed and practiced in numerous ways. With the coming of the Son of God and the eventual working out of the ultimate and perfect sacrifice on the altar of the cross, we see the supreme act to which all other sacrifices in history point. And on that altar, the cross, we see the Sacrifice that imparts meaningfulness to the Old Testament sacrificial system that otherwise seems like so much ritual.

A Savior had been born—born, in fact, to die.

Certain theologians have debated whether Jesus was born the Christ—the prophesied and long-awaited "Anointed One" of Israel, the Messiah—or whether He became the Christ later. But the angels were confident about the truth of it. Actually, the nature of His conception, the angelic annunciation of His birth, the adoration of the Magi and the fear in King Herod (see Matthew 2:1–12) are convincing signals that something out of the ordinary happened that night!

With great confidence the angel announced to the shepherds, "I bring you the gospel of great [Greek, *mega*] joy, and it's for everybody: A Savior has been born to you today; He is Christ the Lord" (Luke 2:10–11, author's paraphrase). And thus were fulfilled the words of Gabriel to Mary that the One to be born would be "the holy one" (Luke 1:35).

There is not a hint of doubt or ambiguity in this angelic communication. Jesus, "the holy one to be born" (Luke 1:35), was Savior and Christ and Lord at birth.

Glory to the newborn King!

7

Jesus: Son of God

"The holy one to be born will be called the Son of God."

Luke 1:35

What the angel Gabriel prophesied—that the holy One, Jesus, would be called the Son of God—had never before been said of the Messiah. Just what does it mean?

The title *Son of God* is an earthly analogy suggesting most strongly the concept of relationship. Because a son inherits the nature of his father, to call someone the Son of God is tantamount in this case to calling Him God.

The writer of Hebrews said that after Jesus ascended into heaven and "sat down at the right hand of the Majesty in heaven . . . he became as much superior to the angels as the name he has inherited is superior to theirs" (1:3–4). What superior name did Jesus inherit? Not *Jesus,* for this name was given by the angel. No, the name Jesus inherited was the one Gabriel said he would be called: *the Son of God.*

According to the writer of Hebrews, God the Father said to Jesus, "You are my Son; today I have become your Father," and, "I will be his Father, and he will be my Son" (1:5).

The incarnation and the Trinity are difficult for the human mind to comprehend because there simply are no earthly counterparts through which we might, by comparison, grasp their meanings. We must rely on the best tools of language available, feeble though they are: figures of speech such as analogies and metaphors.

In the case of the first two Persons of the Trinity, one such figure of speech is the earthly analogy of father and son. This comparison breaks down, however, in the application of our concept of time. On earth the father precedes the son, but it would be a mistake to apply the concept of time to God. Time does not exist in eternity. In the most important area, however, the father-son analogy holds up: the nature of the son, for the son always possesses the same nature as his father.

Thus, when Gabriel prophesied that Jesus would be called the Son of God, he was declaring the deity of Jesus.

Construing this analogy as literal rather than figurative has led various groups into untenable theological positions. The Jehovah's Witnesses, for example, argue by this analogy that Jesus, the Son of God, cannot be God because there is a time when a son, who must come after his father in time, does not exist; and, as we know, God cannot *not* exist. Muslims who take a similar position declare with incredulity that Christians believe God the Father had sexual intercourse with Mary and thus produced the Son of God. Christians believe nothing of the sort, of course, but construe the father-son analogy figuratively, as a symbol of interminable and inextricable relationship. In fact, the Son of God existed as the eternal *Logos* before Jesus was ever conceived (see Genesis 1:26; John 1:1–3). The two natures were joined when Mary conceived—this is the mystery of the incarnation. The *Logos* existed before the conception; the Man Jesus did not.

When a literal interpretation of a passage in the Bible yields an illogical or contrary-to-fact conclusion, the interpreter should consider the possibility that the Scripture under examination is to be taken figuratively. By thus construing the phrase *Son of God,* the nonsensical is eliminated and the meaningful retained.

8

Jesus: The Messiah

"He will be great and will be called the Son of the Most High. The Lord God will give him the throne of his father David, and he will reign over the house of Jacob forever."

Luke 1:32–33

"Today in the town of David [Bethlehem] a Savior has been born to you; he is Christ the Lord."

Luke 2:11

Then one of the elders [angels] said to me, "Do not weep! See, the Lion of the tribe of Judah, the Root of David, has triumphed. He is able to open the scroll and its seven seals."

Revelation 5:5

A Lion, a house, a root, a throne, a town, a tribe, someone named David, someone named Judah, someone named Jacob—what do all these references mean to the twenty-first-century reader? Absolutely nothing—unless he knows something about the Old Testament. Someone once said that the Old Testament is in the New Testament revealed and the New Testament is in the Old Testament concealed. But in the case of these Old Testament allusions, it is the Old Testament that sheds light on the New.

Before we address these obscure allusions, however, we must digress briefly and discuss another pertinent subject: messianic prophecies.

Several hundred years before the birth of Christ, there grew within the Jewish community the belief that God would one day send the Messiah or "Anointed One." (The "anointing" alludes to the ceremonial act of consecrating a prophet, priest or king by pouring oil over him, symbolizing God's presence on him.) The Messiah, it was believed, would establish God's Kingdom on earth and rule with justice and righteousness, defeating God's enemies and ushering in an eternal era of peace for His people.

This insight concerning a coming Messiah was revealed to the Jewish people by the Old Testament prophets, who foretold many things by which the people of God could identify this Messiah. Peter, speaking in the first century A.D. of Jesus' fulfillment of the messianic prophecies, said, "This is how God fulfilled what he had foretold through all the prophets, saying that his Christ would suffer" (Acts 3:18). According to Peter, the prophets of old foretold, by divine inspiration, the coming of the Messiah, and Jesus was the One of whom these prophets spoke.

Thus, the messianic prophecies provided a way for the people of God to identify the Messiah, and this is one way the contemporaries of Jesus identified Him as the Christ. (He was also identified as the Christ by His teachings, His sinless life, His miracles and His resurrection.) We, too, can apply the messianic test to Jesus.

The angelic quotations above attest to Jesus' Messiahship by referring to the lineage from which the Messiah must come and to the place where He had to be born. According to the prophecies of the Old Testament, written hundreds of years before the birth of Jesus, the Messiah would:

Come from the tribe of Judah	Genesis 49:10; Micah 5:2
Come from the royal lineage (root) of King David	Jeremiah 23:5; 2 Samuel 7:12–16; Psalm 132:11
Be born in Bethlehem, the "town of David"	Micah 5:2; 1 Samuel 17:12
Be the Son of God	2 Samuel 7:14; Psalm 2:7
Be called *Lord*	Psalm 110:1

There were other identifying characteristics of the Messiah to which the angels attested. He would be:

A judge	Isaiah 33:22; Acts 10:42 (with 10:22)
A king	Psalm 2:6; Jeremiah 23:5; Luke 1:33; Revelation 17:14
Preceded by a forerunner	Isaiah 40:3; Luke 1:17
Resurrected from the dead	Psalm 16:10; Matthew 28:5–7
Ascended on high	Psalm 68:18; Acts 1:9–11

Interestingly, there is one prophecy in the Old Testament that was spoken by an angel and, five hundred years later in the New Testament, this same angel brought news that would fulfill his own prophecy; he announced the conception of the "Anointed One"—Jesus. The angel was

Gabriel and the prophecy was spoken to Daniel (9:24–26). The prophecy actually foretells the coming of the Messiah, His death and the destruction of the Jewish temple (in A.D. 70).[15]

Someone has compared the prophecies about the coming Messiah to a postal address. Starting with the bottom line and reading upward, an address begins with the broadest location: the state (or country), then the city, then the street, and finally the person's name. Messianic prophecies are somewhat like this. Many are broad, but each additional prophecy eliminates many people, until you are left with just one—the true Messiah.

Here are just a few identifying prophecies with their Old Testament locations and their New Testament fulfillment:

A male child	Genesis 3:15	Galatians 4:4
Seed of Abraham, Isaac and Jacob	Genesis 22:18	Matthew 1:1–2
Son of Isaac	Genesis 21:12	Luke 3:23, 34
Son of Jacob	Numbers 24:17	Luke 3:23, 34
Tribe of Judah	Genesis 49:10	Luke 3:23, 33
Family line of Jesse	Isaiah 11:1	Luke 3:23, 32
Of the house of David	Jeremiah 23:5	Luke 3:23, 31
Born in Bethlehem	Micah 5:2	Matthew 2:1
Born of a virgin	Isaiah 7:14	Matthew 1:18, 24, 25
Preceded by a forerunner	Isaiah 40:3	Matthew 3:1, 2
Betrayed by a friend	Psalm 41:9	Matthew 10:4
Betrayed for thirty pieces of silver	Zechariah 11:12	Matthew 26:15

Hands and feet pierced (crucified)	Psalm 22:16; Zechariah 12:10	Luke 23:33
Buried in a rich man's tomb	Isaiah 53:9	Matthew 27:57–60
Resurrected	Psalm 16:10	Acts 2:31

Only one figure in history lives at this address. His name is Jesus.

"I believe in Jesus Christ, His only Son, our Lord"

The angel's words recorded in Luke 2:10–11 confirm two truths contained in this line of the Apostles' Creed. First, it refers to Jesus as the Christ, a reference to the Old Testament or Hebrew concept of Messiah (translated Christos in the Greek), which means "the Anointed One." The Jews believed that Messiah would be sent from God and come as their great liberator. This concept is also found in the angel's reference to the "town of David." Bethlehem, the birthplace of Jesus, is the "town of David." The Old Testament prophet Micah prophesied 700 years before the birth of Jesus that Messiah would come out of Bethlehem (Micah 5:2).

In Luke 2:10–11 the angel refers to Jesus as the Christ, but also in those verses, the angel refers to Jesus as "Lord." This word is a divine title applied to Jesus. It is also the term that the Jews used to translate the word Adonai, which referred to Yahweh, the name for God that the Jews considered too holy to pronounce or write.

Another messianic prophecy is referred to by the angel Gabriel in his conversation with John the Baptist's father, Zechariah. The angel said of John, "And he will go on before the Lord, in the spirit and power of Elijah, to turn the hearts of the fathers to their children and the disobedient to the wisdom of the righteous—to make ready a people prepared for the Lord" (Luke 1:17). This prophetic utterance about Messiah was uttered originally by the prophet Malachi over 400 years before the birth of Jesus (Malachi 4:5). But more to the point, twice in this verse the angel Gabriel refers to Jesus as "the Lord."

It is true that the word lord was also used as a title of respect for men of position, but it also served as a divine title for God. The words of an angel in Revelation leave no doubt that the reference to Jesus as *Lord* is a reference to Jesus as God: "They will make war against the Lamb, but the Lamb will overcome them because he is Lord of lords and King of kings . . ." (Revelation 17:14).

The titles "Son of God" and "Son of the Most High" are applied to Jesus by the angel Gabriel in his conversation with Mary before her conception: "'He will be great and will be called the Son of the Most High. . . . The Holy Spirit will come upon you, and the power of the Most High will overshadow you. So the holy one to be born will be called the Son of God'" (Luke 1:32, 35).

9

Jesus: Crucified, Dead, Resurrected

The angel said to the women, "Do not be afraid, for I know that you are looking for Jesus, who was crucified. He is not here; he has risen, just as he said. Come and see the place where he lay. Then go quickly and tell his disciples: 'He has risen from the dead and is going ahead of you into Galilee. There you will see him.' Now I have told you."

Matthew 28:5–7

Here an unnamed angel declares several important Christian doctrines.

For hundreds of years non-Christians have tried to explain the empty tomb of Christ. One of several naturalistic theories proposed to "make sense" out of the gospel accounts of the empty grave on Sunday morning is the so-called "swoon theory." This theory posits that Jesus did not really die on the cross; He simply lapsed into unconsciousness. Everyone thought He had died, but in the coolness of the darkened tomb He revived and was declared resurrected.

For nearly fourteen hundred years Muslims have believed that God did not allow Jesus to die on the cross, but removed Him alive and took Him into heaven. To the Muslim mind, Jesus was too great to die. To the Christian, Jesus is great *because* He died, taking on Himself the sins and guilt of the entire human race, becoming the sacrificial Lamb.

A word from the angelic order confirms the truth of this belief. The angel at the empty tomb, who had probably looked in grief and perplexity on the crucifixion, perhaps poised to intervene at his Lord's command (see Matthew 26:53), now declares to the women, "I know you're looking for Jesus, who was crucified. But why do you look for the living among the dead? He's not in the tomb, where He was laid. *He has risen from the dead!* Go to Galilee. You'll see Him there" (see Matthew 28:5–7; Luke 24:5).

The angel even confirms that Jesus prophesied His own death, means of death, and resurrection: "Remember how he told you, while he was still with you in Galilee: 'The Son of Man must be delivered into the hands of sinful men, be crucified and on the third day be raised again'" (Luke 24:6–7). (How did the angel know, incidentally, that Jesus had told His disciples this? He, too, may have been sitting at Jesus' feet—same time, different dimension!)

On the Sunday of Christ's resurrection, two men were walking dejected and downcast on the road from Jerusalem to Emmaus. The man they believed would redeem Israel had been handed over to the Roman authorities "to be sentenced to death, and they crucified him" (Luke 24:20). The two men, who had been joined by a stranger along the way, told him:

> "Some of our women amazed us. They went to the tomb early this morning but didn't find his body. They came and told us that they had seen a vision of angels, who said he was alive. Then some of our companions went to the tomb

and found it just as the women had said, but him they did not see."

verses 22–24

The stranger to whom they had been talking was, in fact, the resurrected Jesus. "Jesus himself came up and walked along with them; but they were kept from recognizing him" (Luke 24:15–16). Eventually, as they reclined and Jesus broke bread, their eyes were opened and they recognized Him. Just then Jesus disappeared, and the two men went immediately back to Jerusalem, found the eleven disciples and testified to the Lord's resurrection (see verses 30–35).

Before Sunday was over, women were telling men and men were telling other men that Jesus had risen from the grave. But it was the angels who started it all. They had first told the women at the empty tomb that "he has risen from the dead" (Matthew 28:7). After all the public shame and disgrace, after the mocking trial and ridicule, after the torturous nails were driven and the spear was thrust, after Jesus had given up the ghost . . . after all this, three days later the angels heralded the unbelievably good news.

The evidence of the angels is too weighty to deny. Jesus died on a cross and rose again.

"Suffered under Pontius Pilate, was crucified, dead and buried; the third day He rose from the dead"

This article of the Creed contains five factual components, all but one explicitly confirmed by the direct utterances of angels.

In Matthew 28:5–6 an angel at the empty tomb confirms that Jesus was crucified, that He was buried ("Come and see the place where he lay," verse 6) and that He rose from the dead.

Luke's account confirms the fourth component of this line of the Creed. In his gospel the angels ask the women who had come to visit the tomb of Jesus:

"Why do you look for the living among the dead? He is not here; he has risen! Remember how he told you, while he was still with you in Galilee: 'The Son of Man must be delivered into the hands of sinful men, be crucified and on the third day be raised again.'"

Luke 24:5–7

Of this article of the Apostles' Creed, only the name of the Roman governor of Judea, Pontius Pilate, is left unspoken by the angels.

"I believe in . . . the resurrection of the body"

The angels of Luke 24:5–6 and Mark 16:6 establish that the tomb is empty, making clear that the resurrection of Jesus was a literal, physical resurrection. So although the Creed speaks here of the raising up of believers, the concept of a bodily resurrection is well established by the utterances of the angels at the empty tomb.

In order to establish that angels also testify to the resurrection of other humans, we have to look at the book that refers most often to the end times, the book of Revelation, for it is not until the end that the general resurrection will occur.

In Revelation 5:9 angelic creatures sing a new song to the Lamb: "With your blood you purchased men for God from every tribe and language and people and nation." The implication is that, being ransomed by and for the eternal God, people will live again eternally. Revelation 11:16–18 also hints of this as the elders "fell on their faces and worshiped God, saying '. . . The time has come for judging the dead, and for rewarding your servants the prophets and your saints and those who reverence your name, both small and great.'"

This discussion seems to confirm that human beings, though they may die, are yet alive. Do they live in a physical, spiritual or some other state? Revelation 5:10 answers this question when the living creatures (angels) and elders conclude their song about the redeemed humans with the following verse: "You have made them to be a kingdom and priests to serve our God, and they will reign on the earth."

I think it is safe to infer that, if the new earth is corporeal, the humans who inhabit it will not be pure spirit beings, mind without body, but will also be corporeal.[16]

10

Jesus: Ascended into Heaven, Returning to Earth

They were looking intently up into the sky as he was going, when suddenly two men dressed in white stood beside them. "Men of Galilee," they said, "why do you stand here looking into the sky? This same Jesus, who has been taken from you into heaven, will come back in the same way you have seen him go into heaven."

Acts 1:10–11

For more than a month after He rose from the dead, Jesus Christ stayed with the apostles. According to Luke's inspired account of the early Church, Jesus stayed with the apostles for forty days, instructing them, speaking to them about the Kingdom of God and demonstrating through "many convincing proofs" that although He had suffered death on the cross, He was indeed alive (Acts 1:1–3).

At the end of those forty days, Jesus was taken up into heaven—not secretly but in plain view of the apostles. So intense, in fact, was their gaze at their ascending Lord that it took two angels to get their attention. Although Scripture states that the apostles were addressed by "two men dressed in white" (Acts 1:10), it is clear that they were angels. They are described as appearing "suddenly"; they are robed in white, like the angels at the empty tomb; they are apparently unknown by any of the apostles; and they are not dumbfounded by the sight of Jesus ascending into clouds. Elsewhere in the book of Acts, Luke calls an angel "a man in shining clothes" (10:30; see 10:3).

The angels tell the apostles that although Jesus has been "taken from you into heaven," He "will come back in the same way" (Acts 1:11).

The second part of the angels' statement seems to be aimed at mitigating the pain of separation reflected in the phrase *taken from you* in the first part of their statement. Had the angels experienced a similar sensation when the *Logos,* the pre-incarnate Christ, left heaven for planet earth?

In any case, we have confirmation from the mouths of angels that Jesus did not remain on the earth, perhaps to die again, nor was He vaporized, nor was His corpse secreted away from or by the apostles. Neither was He leaving never to return. So it is that the utterances of these angels confirm two more cardinal doctrines of Christianity: the ascension and return of Christ to earth.

"He ascended into heaven and sits at the right hand of God the Father Almighty"

The apostles believed that several important events took place after the resurrection of Jesus. Otherwise the movement that Jesus left behind would probably have sputtered, stalled and then taken its modest place in the history books as an obscure Palestinian resurrection cult.

But the account of Jesus in history does not end with the resurrection. In a sense that is only the beginning. As glorious, awe-inspiring and pivotal as the resurrection is, much occurred afterward that was equally important. Forty days after His resurrection Christ ascended from the Mount of Olives near the village of Bethany into the heavenlies. This is what the two angels of Acts confirm: "Jesus has been taken from you into heaven. . . ."

Regarding "sitting on the right hand of the Father," several passages in the book of Revelation describe the angels worshiping Jesus at the throne of God in heaven (see 5:11–14; 7:10–12, 17). In one of these passages, an angel identifies Jesus, the Lamb, "at the center of the throne" (7:17). Evidently this throne is occupied not by one Person of the Trinity but by the fullness of the Godhead, the triune God.[17]

Although the exact creedal phrase *the right hand of the Father* is not used by the angels, it is implied in the Revelation passages, inasmuch as "on the right hand" is figurative imagery indicating the position, power and authority held by Jesus. Six of the eight authors of the New Testament confirm as much. The apostle Peter writes that Jesus "has gone into heaven and is at God's right hand—with angels, authorities and powers in submission to him" (1 Peter 3:22; see Matthew 26:64; Mark 16:19; Luke 22:69; Acts 2:34; Colossians 3:1; Hebrews 12:2).

11

What Fallen Angels Believe about Jesus

When Jesus stepped ashore, he was met by a demon-possessed man from the town. For a long time this man had not worn clothes or lived in a house, but had lived in the tombs. When he saw Jesus, he cried out and fell at his feet, shouting at the top of his voice, "What do you want with me, Jesus, Son of the Most High God? I beg you, don't torture me!"

Luke 8:27–28

It is not unusual to hear friends speak highly of a friend. But when enemies speak highly of an enemy, that calls for pause and consideration. The quotation above is attributed to a demon (verse 27), also known as an evil or unclean spirit (verse 29). (Many theorize that these are fallen angels; see Matthew 12:24–28; 25:41; 2 Peter 2:4; Jude 6; Revelation 12:7–9.) According to this fallen angel, Jesus was the "Son of the Most High God."

Satan, the greatest of all fallen angels, "a guardian cherub" (Ezekiel 28:14), "the god of this age" (2 Corinthians 4:4) and "prince of this world" (John 12:31), acknowledged the same truth about Jesus when he tempted Him during His desert fast: "If you are the Son of God . . ." (Matthew 4:1–6; Luke 4:3–9). In the same way, Satan assumed the existence of God when he tempted Eve in the Garden of Eden: "Did God really say . . ." (Genesis 3:1). The fallen angels never dispute the existence of God; in fact, James 2:19 says the demons believe in one God—"and shudder." Similarly the fallen angels recognized Jesus. "I know who you are," one of them blurted out to Jesus (Luke 4:34) before being cast out.

In one of the most memorable exorcisms in the Bible, seven sons of a Jewish chief priest were using the names of Jesus and Paul (who preached Jesus) to cast a demon out of a man.

> The evil spirit answered them, "Jesus I know, and I know about Paul, but who are you?" Then the man who had the evil spirit jumped on them and overpowered them all. He gave them such a beating that they ran out of the house naked and bleeding.
>
> Acts 19:15–16

That the demons knew who Jesus was may not seem very important, but inasmuch as these demons, speaking through the mouths of those they possessed, could be heard by others around them, they could utilize their knowledge about Jesus to disrupt the intricate timing of God's plan of salvation for the earth. For this reason Jesus had to order them at times, "Be quiet!" (Mark 1:25; Luke 4:35). In one encounter a fallen angel said, "I know who you are—the Holy One of God!" (Mark 1:24). On another occasion "demons came out of many people, shouting, 'You are the Son of God!' But he rebuked them and would not allow them to speak, because they knew he was the Christ" (Luke 4:41).

According to Duane Garrett in *Angels and the New Spirituality,* the demons in Luke 4:41 "could not refrain from shouting out, 'You are the Son of God!' The text implies that, being spiritual entities, they could not fail to acknowledge the presence of God among them."[18] It also seems that the demons knew their ultimate fate and the power and authority of Jesus, for they asked Him, "Have you come here to torture us before the appointed time?" (Matthew 8:29). And, "What do you want with us, Jesus of Nazareth? Have you come to destroy us?" (Mark 1:24). And, "What do you want with me, Jesus, Son of the Most High God? Swear to God that you won't torture me!" (Mark 5:7). The demons "begged him repeatedly not to order them to go into the Abyss" (Luke 8:31; see Revelation 20:1–3).

Interestingly, it seems that all the titles applied to Jesus by Gabriel at Christ's conception were known and used by the fallen angels, too. Observe the following parallels:

Gabriel	**Fallen Angels**
Jesus (Luke 1:31) (Luke 8:28; Mark 1:24)	Jesus/Jesus of Nazareth
Son of God (Luke 1:35)	Son of God (Luke 4:41)
Holy one (Luke 1:35)	Holy One of God (Mark 1:24)
Son of the Most High (Luke 1:32)	Son of the Most High God (Mark 5:7; Luke 8:28)

No fallen angel ever accused Jesus of being less than who He really is, although Satan used that tactic when he tried to tempt Jesus (see Matthew 4:1–11). Instead they addressed Him as deity and begged Him to have mercy on them (Mark 5:7, 10, 12; Luke 8:31).

With the crucifixion of Jesus, the fallen angels perhaps thought they had thwarted God's plan to save humankind. But now they know that God's plan to save humanity was, in fact, gloriously effected through the very act the demons meant for the greatest of all evils—the death of Jesus on the cross, which instead became the saving sacrifice of the Lamb of God.

In the book of Acts a slave girl possessed by a spirit followed Paul and his entourage continuously, shouting, "These men are servants of the Most High God, who are telling you *the way to be saved*" (16:17, emphasis added). Finally Paul, tired of this girl's hounding and shrieking, turned on her and addressed the evil spirit: "'In the name of Jesus Christ I command you to come out of her!' At that moment the spirit left her" (verse 18). This exorcism led to Paul's imprisonment, which led to the salvation of the jailer, who asked Paul and Silas, "'Sirs, what must I do to be saved?' They replied, 'Believe in the Lord Jesus, and you will be saved—you and your household'" (verses 30–31).

The words of the possessed servant girl indicate that fallen angels are aware of the effectiveness of Christ's death on the cross and the commitment of Christians to their Lord, for the evil spirit called Paul and the others "servants of the Most High God." Would that every Christian could be so recognized! Even as the evil spirit could say, "Jesus I know and Paul I know," so believers living in the Spirit and fulfilling the call of God in their lives should be recognized by evil spirits, who say, "Jesus I know and Paul I know *and you I know!*"

Make it so, Holy Spirit.

Part 2

Rejoicing at Their Salvation

What Angels Believe about Humankind

The ministry of angels to humans is one of the great secrets of our time. It reminds me of the old adage "Out of sight, out of mind." We cannot see angels unless they are unveiled by God, so their presence goes largely unrecognized and unappreciated. Yet the Scriptures are replete with their involvement in human affairs. Jesus indicates that children (at least) have "personal" angels to care for them, and that angels may even get a bit emotional about human beings, rejoicing over each one who comes, as a child, to God.

The angels are not ignorant of the plight of humans, nor are they apathetic. If they rejoice at our repentance, do they mourn over our rebellion? The Bible reveals angels working feverishly to implement the plan of God for the benefit of humankind. What they say about us, then, should pique our interest.

This section reveals great truths that angels have spoken about humankind.

12

Caution! Angels at Work

When Men and Women Pray

"As soon as you began to pray, an answer was given. . . ."

Daniel 9:23

Prayer occurs when humans, in reverence, address God. When we think of prayer, normally we think of requesting something of Him—perhaps food for the hungry, protection for loved ones, salvation for the lost, guidance for a decision or a miracle for a hopeless situation. Several times in the Old and New Testaments, angels mention the prayers of humans. And in two passages in the book of Daniel, angels were the agents God used to answer prayer.

On one occasion the angel Gabriel appeared to Daniel and said, "I have now come to give you insight and understanding. As soon as you began to pray, an answer was given, which I have come to tell you, for you are highly esteemed" (Daniel 9:22–23).

Another time the archangel Michael played a role in the answering of Daniel's prayer. An angel (perhaps Gabriel) was attempting to deliver God's answer to Daniel's prayer when he was intercepted and detained in battle by a fallen angel. As the angel explained to Daniel:

> "Do not be afraid, Daniel. Since the first day that you set your mind to gain understanding and to humble yourself before your God, your words were heard, and I have come in response to them. But the prince of the Persian kingdom [a fallen angel] resisted me twenty-one days. Then [the archangel] Michael, one of the chief princes, came to help me, because I was detained there with the king of Persia."
>
> Daniel 10:12–13

It is noteworthy that on both occasions of prayer, the Scriptures say God heard Daniel's prayers *immediately:* "As soon as you began to pray" and "Since the first day . . . your words were heard." There is no reason to think that the effectiveness of our own prayers or the speed of God's responses today is different.

Zechariah, father of John the Baptist, was told by an angel prior to his son's birth, "Your prayer has been heard. Your wife Elizabeth will bear you a son, and you are to give him the name John" (Luke 1:13). Much later the Roman commander Cornelius was told by an angel, "Your prayers and gifts to the poor have come up as a memorial offering before God" (Acts 10:4). Thus it is apparent that angels are instrumental at times in conveying to men and women God's answer to their prayers.

Furthermore, a passage in Revelation implies that angels have also been the means of conveying *to God* the prayers of humans. The apostle John describes the following scene from a vision he experienced in the Spirit: "The smoke of the incense, together with the prayers of the saints, went up before God from the angel's hand" (Revelation 8:4). This is reminiscent of the angelic visitation to Samson's parents, when "the angel of the LORD ascended in the flame" of the altar fire (Judges 13:20).

It is true that the books of Daniel and Revelation are visionary and, as such, highly symbolic. We should not, therefore, draw hasty conclusions based solely on such passages. We must also understand, however, that the symbolism in a visionary passage, while elevating the language beyond the literal, does not contradict the literal by use of the symbolic; it is, in fact, exalting a truth too great to be contained in and conveyed by the literal. For this reason symbolic language should not be interpreted literally but carried to a higher plane. To do otherwise is to allow the mundane to rob the sublime.

Whatever the connection between angels and prayer, this we know: God hears and answers the prayers of humans, sometimes using angels.

Having said this, I must also point out that in the Scriptures, angels are never the recipients or addressees of prayers. To God alone are we to pray. In reply to the direct request, "Teach us to pray," Jesus said, "You should pray like this: Our Father in heaven . . ." (Matthew 6:9, CEV). Jesus also said, "When you pray, go into your room, close the door and pray to your Father . . ." (Matthew 6:6). Paul instructed Christians, "In everything, by prayer and petition, with thanksgiving, present your requests to God" (Philippians 4:6). Elsewhere he criticized those engaging in "the worship of angels" (Colossians 2:18; see also 2 Corinthians 11:14; Galatians 1:8; 1 Timothy 4:1). Jesus told His disciples that when He returned to the Father, they could address Him in prayer as well: "You may ask me for anything in my name, and I will do it" (John 14:14).

Duane Garrett asks incredulously, "Could Christians prefer praying to angels over calling on the name of Jesus?"[19] Later he makes this astute observation:

Whatever an angel is, one thing is certain: an angel is not human. To call upon an angel when you need food is to call upon someone who has never felt the pangs of hunger. To call upon an angel when you are sick is to call upon someone who has never known sickness. To seek an angel's comfort when mourning the death of a friend is to call upon one who has never known grief or death.

Jesus, on the other hand, has known what it was to breathe the quiet air of an early Galilean morning. He has felt what it is to work with His hands and no doubt experienced the frustration of a piece of wood that just would not fit where it was supposed to. He was carried in His mother's arms. He has felt the pain of an empty stomach and has heard the tempter's voice telling Him to take a moral shortcut to sate that hunger. He has heard the singing and the celebration of a wedding party, and He has been in a house of mourning, when a little daughter was taken by death. Jesus has wept.

. . . I do not know if tears have ever stained an angel's face, but I know that they have stained His. Jesus did drink deeply from the cup of sorrow; it did not pass from Him. That cup has never been near an angel's lips.[20]

13

We May Be Filled with the Holy Spirit

"He [John the Baptist] will be filled with the Holy Spirit even from birth."

Luke 1:15

It would be helpful if the angels had said more about being filled with the Holy Spirit, since this applies to human beings and since the Bible represents it as an incredibly awesome phenomenon.

For John the Baptist, being filled with the Holy Spirit was associated with his prophesied mission of living "in the spirit and power of Elijah" and turning the hearts of people back to God and to their families (Luke 1:17). Just before the angel told Zechariah that his son would be filled with the Spirit, he told him that John was "never to take wine or other fermented drink" (verse 15).

Two references in the New Testament compare the experience of being filled with the Holy Spirit to drinking wine. On the Day of Pentecost the believers filled with the Spirit were accused of being drunk (Acts 2:15). Later Paul exhorted the Christians in Ephesus (Greece) not to get drunk with wine but to "be filled with the Spirit" (Ephesians 5:18). Both of these references imply that being filled with the Spirit may result in the believer's entering an impassioned state—under the influence of the Spirit, however, and not strong drink. Perhaps John the Baptist was reared to abstain from strong drink because of his intense passion and zeal for God and godliness, lest it be credited for the fire and fervor in his bones.

It is while we are under the influence of the Spirit that mighty things happen—things that otherwise could not come about, no matter what human resources are available.

An angel's words to Zerubbabel make this exact point. Zerubbabel, a prince of Judah and governor of Jerusalem, was commissioned by God to rebuild the holy Temple in Jerusalem. When his plans were met with opposition and hostilities, an angel delivered this message through the prophet Zechariah: "This is the word of the LORD to Zerubbabel: 'Not by might nor by power, but by my Spirit,' says the LORD Almighty" (4:6). The arm of the Lord is greater than all the armies of men.

Both Old and New Testaments are replete with marvelous accounts of men and women submitting themselves to the influence of the Spirit of God. The book of Acts is a good place to start for those interested in studying more about the Spirit-filled life.

"I believe in the Holy Spirit"

The word *Spirit* or *Holy Spirit* is used by the angels on at least four occasions. Three are related to the incarnation of Jesus. Of these three, two are directly linked to Jesus' conception (see Matthew 1:20; Luke 1:35) and the third is connected to John the Baptist, who was (as we have seen) "filled with the Holy Spirit even from birth" (Luke 1:15).

The fourth angelic use of the word *Spirit* is found in the Old Testament book of Zechariah. There, as quoted earlier, an unnamed angel tells the prophet, "'Not by might nor by power, but by my Spirit,' says the LORD Almighty" (4:6). The angel's message is meant to encourage Zerubbabel, whom God had called to rebuild the Jewish Temple. It would not be human ingenuity or strength that restored the Temple, but God Himself.

14

The Bridegroom Returns for His Bride

"Let us rejoice and be glad and give him glory! For the wedding of the Lamb has come, and his bride has made herself ready."

Revelation 19:7

The imagery of God or Christ as the Bridegroom and the Church as the bride is found four times in the book of Revelation (19:7; 21:2, 9; 22:17). These symbols point to the bridegroom's return to the bride's home for the culmination of the marriage ceremony.

It was customary in first-century Palestine for the bridegroom (in this case, Christ) to visit the bride's home (earth). Then would come a time of separation during which the bride and groom were considered betrothed— that is, husband and wife. The groom would then return to the bride's home and take her to his own home (the New Jerusalem or, in effect, heaven).

In chapter 10 we saw that the angels believe Jesus is coming back to earth. In the highly symbolic book of Revelation, it is evident that Jesus' return will be a glorious and epochal event. In Acts 1:11 the angels tell us that Jesus will return to earth, but the Revelation passages tell us *why* He is returning: He is returning for His bride. An angel declares, "Blessed are those who are invited to the wedding supper of the Lamb!" (Revelation 19:9).

It is clear from Revelation 21:9–27 why the angel pronounces the attendees "blessed," for no human has ever been able to match the angel's incredible revelation of the New Jerusalem coming down from heaven, created for the children of God! The best man can offer is, "No eye has seen, no ear has heard, no mind has conceived what God has prepared for those who love him," the apostle Paul writes, paraphrasing the prophet Isaiah (1 Corinthians 2:9; see Isaiah 64:4).

Happily we have the eyewitness testimony of a being from the realm of the heavenlies to give us a glimpse of the coming new world. Who, after all, could be more qualified than an angel to reveal heaven's grandeur?

> "Come, I will show you the bride, the wife of the Lamb."
> And he . . . showed me the Holy City, Jerusalem, coming
> down out of heaven from God. It shone with the glory of
> God, and its brilliance was like that of a very precious jewel,
> like a jasper, clear as crystal. It had a great, high wall with
> twelve gates, and with twelve angels at the gates. . . . The
> foundations of the city walls were decorated with every
> kind of precious stone. The first foundation was jasper, the
> second sapphire, the third chalcedony, the fourth emerald, the fifth sardonyx, the sixth carnelian, the seventh
> chrysolite, the eighth beryl, the ninth topaz, the tenth
> chrysoprase, the eleventh jacinth, and the twelfth amethyst. The twelve gates were twelve pearls, each gate made
> of a single pearl. The great street of the city was of pure
> gold, like transparent glass. I did not see a temple in the

city, because the Lord God Almighty and the Lamb are its temple. The city does not need the sun or the moon to shine on it, for the glory of God gives it light, and the Lamb is its lamp. . . . Nothing impure will ever enter it, nor will anyone who does what is shameful or deceitful, but only those whose names are written in the Lamb's book of life.

Revelation 21:9–12, 19–23, 27

The holy angels of God believe in the bride of Christ, the Church, and the triumphant, end-time celebration of the Marriage Supper of the Lamb. All of humankind, according to the Scriptures, is invited: "For God so loved the world that he gave his one and only Son, that whoever believes in him shall not perish but have eternal life" (John 3:16). "The Lord is not slow in keeping his promise, as some understand slowness. He is patient with you, not wanting anyone to perish, but everyone to come to repentance" (2 Peter 3:9). God "wants all men to be saved and to come to a knowledge of the truth" (1 Timothy 2:4). Unfortunately not all will believe and come to repentance, but for those who do, a celebration of eternal life awaits.

Will you welcome the Second Coming of Christ as it is heralded by the archangel Michael (see 1 Thessalonians 4:16)? The angels want you to be there for "there is rejoicing in [their] presence" over every human who comes to God (Luke 15:10).

"I believe in . . . the holy catholic Church; the communion of the saints"

The word *church* is used to translate the Greek word *ekklesia*, which originally meant an assembly or body of people. Before the New Testament was completed (and probably before it was begun), the word had taken on this technical sense of Christian believers; and in the great majority of occurrences in the New Testament (112 out of

115), it refers to either a local body of Christians or the universal Christian population, the complete Body of Christ.

Although the angels do not use the word *church,* they refer in several New Testament passages to the body of believers. In Revelation 5:9–10 the angel mentions those who were ransomed for God by the blood of Christ. Note that these were not "every tribe and language and people and nation"; they were *"from* every tribe and language and people and nation" (verse 9). They are those who make up the Church universal.

The angels also refer to the "saints" (Revelation 16:6; 18:20), which is a general term for all who have been set apart from the profane and consecrated to God. Please understand that the meaning of *saint* is a far cry from the pedestrian concept of a perfect person. To paraphrase a popular bumper sticker, a saint is not perfect, just forgiven. Through forgiveness the perfection of Christ has been imputed to each believer, and *His* holiness has become *their* holiness.

It is this imputation that brings the new nature Paul speaks of when he writes, "We serve in the new way of the Spirit, and not in the old way of the written code" (Romans 7:6), and, "Since we live by the Spirit, let us keep in step with the Spirit" (Galatians 5:25; see also 1 Corinthians 15:45–49). This sharing of the new nature is what brings about the communion of the saints.

Finally the angels refer to the group of believers as the *bride* of the Lamb, the wife (Revelation 19:7; 21:9). One angel says the bride was given "fine linen, bright and clean . . . to wear," and John explains that "fine linen stands for the righteous acts of the saints" (Revelation 19:8). The implication: that believers are to live by a greater ethical standard than the world. So even though our holiness is in Christ, our acts are to serve as a reflection of our God.

15

Man and the Coming End-Time Judgment

I saw another angel flying in midair, and he had the eternal gospel to proclaim to those who live on the earth—to every nation, tribe, language and people. He said in a loud voice, "Fear God and give him glory, because the hour of his judgment has come. Worship him who made the heavens, the earth, the sea and the springs of water."

Revelation 14:6–7

There is good, according to the Scriptures, and there is evil; there is right and there is wrong. Each human has been given the freedom and power to choose which he or she will do. Either choice has its consequences, both in this present world and in the world to come. Concerning the relationship of our present choices to eternal consequences, one theologian has phrased it succinctly: "Right now counts forever."

The angels would agree. In fact, Jesus tells us, "This is how it will be at the end of the age. The angels will come and separate the wicked from the righteous and throw them into the fiery furnace, where there will be weeping and gnashing of teeth" (Matthew 13:49–50).

In the book of Revelation, too, the angels play an instrumental role in the end-time judgment of humankind. One angel calls in a loud voice to another who has come from heaven: "Take your sharp sickle and gather the clusters of grapes from the earth's vine, because its grapes are ripe" (14:18). Then, in the vision, John is shown the result: "The angel swung his sickle on the earth, gathered its grapes and threw them into the great winepress of God's wrath. They were trampled in the winepress outside the city, and blood flowed out of the press, rising as high as the horses' bridles for a distance of 1,600 stadia [184 miles]" (verses 19–20).

Angels are often portrayed as gentle, loving and protecting beings, and sometimes they are all of these. But it is not for nothing that the psalmist calls them "destroying angels" (78:49). God will not endure evil forever; His justice cries out for satisfaction and fulfillment. A time is coming when He will put an end to all wickedness. And in His end-time extinguishing of evil, angels will play a role, as further revealed in Revelation 14:

> A third angel followed them and said in a loud voice: "If anyone worships the beast and his image and receives his mark on the forehead or on the hand, he, too, will drink of the wine of God's fury, which has been poured full strength into the cup of his wrath. He will be tormented with burning sulfur in the presence of the holy angels and of the Lamb. And the smoke of their torment rises for ever and ever. There is no rest day or night for those who worship the beast and his image, or for anyone who receives the mark of his name."
>
> verses 9–11

Even as God is infinite and eternal, so are His laws. They are in some inscrutable way extensions of His nature. And as a corollary, transgression of and rebellion against those laws call for punishment that is infinite and eternal, because, in James Sire's words, it "is profoundly evil to reject the profoundly good."[21]

The good news is that the bliss of God's Kingdom is also infinite and eternal. "Nothing impure will ever enter it," according to the angel of Revelation 21:27, "nor will anyone who does what is shameful or deceitful, but only those whose names are written in the Lamb's book of life."

The creatures whom God gave the freedom to choose between obedience and rebellion chose rebellion—an act for which a price had to be paid. How marvelous is God's love: *He paid the price Himself!* While other religions tell adherents to "Do, do, do," Christianity tells everyone, "Done!" As the song goes, "We owed a debt we could not pay" while Jesus, on the cross, "paid a debt He did not owe." But the satisfaction of the debt applies only to those who choose to believe and follow Christ.

All may choose!

"From thence he shall come to judge the living and the dead"

When Luke penned the words, "This same Jesus . . . will come back in the same way you have seen him go into heaven" (Acts 1:11), he was recording an angelic validation of the first part of the article now at hand: "Whence he comes. . . ." According to the Creed, Jesus, who is now with the Father in heaven, will come again. Likewise the angels state that the Son of God, though He has ascended into heaven, will one day return to earth.

Later the angel spoke to Cornelius and told him that Peter "will bring you a message through which you and all your household will be saved" (Acts 11:14). Part of Peter's message was this: Jesus "is the one whom God appointed as judge of the living and the dead" (Acts 10:42).

These words of Peter were validated once again by angelic witnesses in the book of Revelation. An angel said, "Fear God and give him glory, because the hour of his judgment has come" (14:7). Revelation 6 describes Jesus and the angels as being integrally involved in the seven seals of judgment unleashed in the end times. Thus it would seem that the angels in Revelation consider Jesus the Judge of the end times—incidentally affirming this article of the Creed.

"I believe in . . . the life everlasting"

By nature angels are acclimated to a timeless existence. Nowhere in Scripture do we read of angels growing old and dying, which is reasonable since they are incorporeal spirit beings, without possession of the fleshly bodies we know only too well.

Here is good news: A time will come, according to the angels, when humankind will experience an eternal state. Such is described by an angel in Revelation 7:15: "They [who have come out of the great tribulation] are before the throne of God and serve him day and night in his temple" (Revelation 7:15). In fact, the angel goes on to say of redeemed humankind: "Never again will they hunger; never again will they thirst. The sun will not beat upon them, nor any scorching heat. For the Lamb at the center of the throne will be their shepherd; he will lead them to springs of living water. And God will wipe away every tear from their eyes" (verses 16–17).

In Revelation 17:8 an angel speaks of "the book of life," also called the Lamb's Book of Life. (The word *Life* in the title refers to everlasting life.) In it are written the names of believers who have accepted Christ's atoning sacrifice as satisfaction for their own sins. In the last chapter of Revelation an angel shows John the eternal city of God, inhabited by those whose names are written in the Book of Life. Here is what the angel reveals to John:

Then the angel showed me the river of the water of life, as clear as crystal, flowing from the throne of God and of the Lamb down the middle of the great street of the city. On each side of the river stood the tree of life, bearing twelve crops of fruit, yielding its fruit every month. And the leaves of the tree are for the healing of the nations.

No longer will there be any curse. The throne of God and of the Lamb will be in the city, and his servants will serve him. They will see his face, and his name will be on their foreheads. There will be no more night. They will not need the light of a lamp or the light of the sun, for the Lord God will give them light. And they will reign for ever and ever.

Revelation 22:1–5

16

The Angels' View of Human Sin

"This is the iniquity of the people throughout the land. . . .
This is wickedness."

Zechariah 5:6, 8

"He will save his people from their sins."

Matthew 1:21

Angels are not ignorant about evil or sin. After all, evil existed in their realm before the earth was created. In fact, the origin of evil is traceable to an angelic creature (see Genesis 3; Isaiah 14; 2 Peter 2:4; Jude 6), after which it found its way to humankind. The angel quoted in Zechariah 5:6, 8 speaks of iniquity and wickedness. In Matthew 1:21 the angel Gabriel says Jesus "will save his people from their sins." Another angel acknowledges that "sinful men" crucified Jesus (Luke 24:7). And a seraph, an angelic being, tells Isaiah, "Your guilt is taken away and your sin atoned for" (6:7).

Angels are aware, then, of the sinfulness of man and God's attitude toward human sin. They are equally aware of His provisions for humankind to cure the problem of sin, which stands as an insuperable spiritual barrier between unholy humankind and the holy Creator.

If the difference between Creator and creation is already unfathomable, how much more distance does man's disobedience put between himself and God? And how is man, the creature, to solve his predicament? How is he even to know he is in a predicament? How can he understand the mind of the Creator or know what to do to reconcile himself to God? He cannot, of course. For a person to think otherwise is to scale the mountain of presumption and crown himself God. Then his end is worse than his beginning, for at that point he is not only sinful but deluded.

If reconciliation is to occur, God must take the initiative, bridging the gap and revealing Himself and His ways to humankind. For this reason Jesus came into the world. An angel (probably Gabriel since he had a special ministry related to the mystery of the incarnation) told Jesus' adoptive earthly father, Joseph, that Mary "will give birth to a son, and you are to give him the name Jesus, because he will save his people from their sins" (Matthew 1:21).

On another occasion (mentioned in the last chapter), an angel appeared to Cornelius, a Roman soldier, who would become the first recorded Gentile convert to Christianity. The angel told him to send to the port city of Joppa (Palestine) for a man named Peter, and "he will bring you a message through which you and all your household will be saved" (Acts 11:14). The heavenly messenger was directing Cornelius on how to obtain divine knowledge about salvation. Here is Peter's message to the Gentiles:

> You know what has happened throughout Judea, beginning in Galilee after the baptism that John preached— how God anointed Jesus of Nazareth with the Holy Spirit

and power, and how he went around doing good and healing all who were under the power of the devil, because God was with him. We are witnesses of everything he did in the country of the Jews and in Jerusalem. They killed him by hanging him on a tree, but God raised him from the dead on the third day and caused him to be seen. He was not seen by all the people, but by witnesses whom God had already chosen—by us who ate and drank with him after he rose from the dead. . . . All the prophets testify about him that everyone who believes in him receives forgiveness of sins through his name.

Acts 10:37–41, 43

Thus, humans are "saved" through the forgiveness of sins. But how does Jesus forgive sin? What did He do to effect the forgiveness of sin and provide salvation for man?

Six months before Mary became pregnant with Jesus, an angel appeared to John the Baptist's father-to-be and told him that his wife, Elizabeth, would bear him a son. This son, said the angel, would "go on before the Lord, in the spirit and power of Elijah, to turn the hearts of the fathers to their children and the disobedient to the wisdom of the righteous—to make ready a people prepared for the Lord" (Luke 1:17). Part of preparing a people for the Lord would include introducing them to Jesus. Indeed: "John saw Jesus coming toward him and said, 'Look, the Lamb of God, who takes away the sin of the world!'" (John 1:29).

Curiously, angels in heaven also refer to Jesus as *the Lamb*. In the book of Revelation the angels sing in a loud voice, "Worthy is the Lamb, who was slain, to receive power and wealth and wisdom and strength and honor and glory and praise!" (5:12). Two chapters later the apostle John is shown in a vision a great multitude dressed in white robes "from every nation, tribe, people and language" (7:9). An angel tells John, "These are they who have come out of the great tribulation; they have washed their robes and made them white in the blood of the Lamb" (verse 14).

I opened the previous paragraph with the word *curiously*. I hope it caught your attention. It is curious that angels in heaven refer to Jesus as *the Lamb* because that metaphor can have no special meaning for them. The title *Lamb of God* is a reference to God's covenant of sacrifice *with humankind* that is found first in the Old Testament, where it is a precursor or foreshadowing of the sacrificial offering of Jesus, the Lamb of God, on the altar of the cross. Both Paul and Peter refer to Jesus as the Lamb. Paul tells the Christians at Corinth that "Christ, our Passover lamb, has been sacrificed" (1 Corinthians 5:7) and Peter refers to Jesus as "a lamb without blemish or defect" (1 Peter 1:19).

There is nothing magical, mystical or supernatural about the sacrificial system. The elaborate rituals of sacrifices found in the Old Testament are, without the impartation of significance by God Himself, spiritually empty. They are meaningful solely because God gives them meaning, and He does this in two ways. First He does it by divine fiat. He is the Creator; we are the creation. He may do as He pleases. Second, and more important, Jesus stooped, He bowed, He "emptied himself" (Philippians 2:7, RSV), becoming the perfect sacrifice through incarnation and crucifixion. He became our reconciler and mediator.

The less one knows of love, the less one understands this. It is the most incredibly wonderful truth of the Bible: "This is love: not that we loved God, but that he loved us and sent his Son as an atoning sacrifice for our sins" (1 John 4:10).

The seemingly crude and primitive ritual of sacrifice in the Old Testament was but a shadow of the substance, and although only a blip on the screen of the eons, the death of Jesus on the cross would affect all of eternity. We find the first hint of its timelessness in Revelation 13:8, where

Jesus is described as "the Lamb that was slain from the creation of the world." The book of Revelation, a prophetic book that *reveals* (hence its title) the future of those "whose names are written in the Lamb's book of life" (21:27), refers to Jesus as *the Lamb* 26 times. (There are only 31 such references in all of the New Testament.) In this book we are shown a picture of heaven, the city of God, of which it is said, "The Lord God Almighty and the Lamb are its temple. The city does not need the sun or the moon to shine on it, for the glory of God gives it light, and the Lamb is its lamp" (21:22–23).

Through the course of time, within the history of the lineage of one man, God's progressive revelation of Himself culminated in a clear picture of this God of personal love. The truth is humbling: The cure for humankind's problem of sin is found in the One he sinned against. God's righteous Son made the way; He became the door. Man has only to believe and follow this God of inexhaustible, inexorable love.

Through the fall of the human race, an attribute of God was surfacing—an attribute that might otherwise never have been known. Defining itself in the darkness of human debauchery—bursting through hate, rebellion, disobedience, unbelief—surfacing irresistibly, with the certainty and sureness of a bubble dislodged from the ocean floor, was . . . *the love of God!*

"I believe in . . . the forgiveness of sins"

I have devoted chapters 6 and 16 of this book to the angelic utterances that relate to human sinfulness and the cure in Jesus, the Holy One who saves from sin through forgiveness. Four other chapters speak implicitly to this topic. The forgiveness of sin is perhaps the greatest theme of Christianity. Contrary to the adversaries of Christianity, who paint it as narrow and bigoted, it is a faith that opens wide the gateway to God by offering forgiveness and spiritual healing to all who will come.

Angels speak explicitly of human sin, iniquity or wickedness in both Old and New Testaments (see Zechariah 3:3–4; 5:6; Matthew 1:21; Revelation 18:4). And indirectly an angel confirms Christ's authority to forgive sin when Peter, in a sermon certified by an angel (see Acts 11:13–14), preaches that "everyone who believes in [Jesus] receives forgiveness of sins through his name" (Acts 10:43).

17

What Angels Believe about Mary

The angel went to her and said, "Greetings, you who are highly favored! The Lord is with you. . . . Do not be afraid, Mary, you have found favor with God."

Luke 1:28, 30

Very few people have been blessed with a visible angelic visitation. Interestingly, and understandably, those in Scripture who have are often told by the angel, "Do not be afraid" (see Genesis 21:17; Daniel 10:12; Matthew 28:5; Mark 16:6; Luke 1:13, 30; 2:10). In Luke's account of Mary's visitation by Gabriel, we learn that "Mary was greatly troubled at his words and wondered what kind of greeting this might be" (1:29). Gabriel had simply said to her, "Greetings, you who are highly favored! The Lord is with you."

In retrospect we might even consider the angel's words an understatement. Of the billions of women who would inhabit the earth, only one would be chosen to bear the promised Messiah, the incarnation of God. The greeting *The Lord is with you* turned out to be a double entendre with an even more important and special meaning. Mary herself would become holy ground.[22] Within Mary's womb the Savior would be nurtured; from her womb would come the Messiah, humankind's Redeemer. As her water broke and her baby emerged into human history, the stream of earth's time would split in two—B.C. and A.D.

Blessed she is among women and highly favored of God. Gabriel, straight from God to Mary, would tell her:

> "You will be with child and give birth to a son, and you are to give him the name Jesus. He will be great and will be called the Son of the Most High. The Lord God will give him the throne of his father David, and he will reign over the house of Jacob forever; his kingdom will never end."

Luke 1:31–33

The incredible, absolute awe of this passed right over Mary's head at first as she pondered the more personal and practical question, "How will this be . . . since I am a virgin?" (verse 34).

As the name of the Messiah, *Jesus*, was uttered first by the lips of Gabriel, it fell first on the ears of His mother, Mary. How precious it must have sounded, and how fitting that the first on earth to hear the Messiah's name spoken was the mother who would bear Him, nurture Him and present Him to the world.

Part 3

Words You Can Trust

What Angels Believe about the Bible

We call them *angels*—those heavenly, spiritual beings who deliver messages between God and humankind. They do much more, of course, but so important is this duty that their proper name is derived from the Hebrew and Greek words for *messenger*. Many of their messages have been inscripturated into the revealed, written revelation we know as the Bible.

Add to their duty of heralds their superior intellect, their holiness and their face-to-face experience with the Creator, and you have a faithful witness to God and His revealed truth. Given this portfolio, whom could we trust more than angels to hold the proper perspective of God's written revelation to humankind?

Thus the words of angels about the Word of God hold special interest for human ears. This section looks into these angelic words.

18

"The Bible Tells Me So"

Truth and Scripture

"These are the true words of God."

Revelation 19:9

Any discussion of divine revelation or sacred Scriptures must of necessity involve the issue of *truth*—more so for our times than for any other, since many people believe that truth is either unattainable or, in the end, relative, especially concerning moral matters. Assuming that the seeker of truth survives these pitfalls, he must then face the issue of whether truth can be conveyed through the medium of language—spoken and written.

The angels were neither tentative nor reluctant about conveying the words of God via human language. Evidently they believed the truth was neither lost nor corrupted in the translation process; otherwise the angel would not have told the apostle John to write down his words and then declared, "These are the true words of God."

It interests me that God, through this angel, would describe His words as "true." By definition the words of God cannot be false, making it redundant to describe them as true. I can only surmise that God was speaking for the benefit of those humans who would give greater heed to language so couched, or else He was making a clear distinction between these words and words attributed to Him by false prophets. If the former supposition is true, we might paraphrase the sentence this way: "These are the words of God; thus they must be true." If the latter supposition is true, we might paraphrase it this way: "These are the words of God, which are true, as opposed to the words of false prophets."

Either way, the angel rebuts the notion that spiritual truth cannot be communicated from God to humankind through the medium of human language. This one sentence confirms what theologians call *propositional revelation,* and it proves beyond question that God speaks to humankind and reveals Himself and His will to man. Incidentally, if God does this, going to the trouble of communicating, we can safely conclude that He must care about His creation.

An angel speaking to the apostle John clearly indicates his belief in the trustworthiness and validity of written prophecies and in the Judeo-Christian prophetic tradition:

> The angel said to me, "These words are trustworthy and true. The Lord, the God of the spirits of the prophets, sent his angel to show his servants the things that must soon take place." . . . I, John, am the one who heard and saw these things. And when I had heard and seen them, I fell down to worship at the feet of the angel who had been showing them to me. But he said to me, "Do not do it! I am a fellow servant with you and with your brothers the prophets and of all who keep the words of this book. Wor-

ship God!" Then he told me, "Do not seal up the words of the prophecy of this book, because the time is near."

Revelation 22:6, 8–10

The angel verifies two things: the end product—that is, the book and its individual words; and also the supernatural vehicle, the spirit of prophecy. Jesus Himself puts His stamp of approval on it: "I, Jesus, have sent my angel to give you this testimony for the churches" (verse 16).

In the Old Testament an angel tells the prophet Zechariah, "Proclaim this word: This is what the LORD Almighty says . . ." (1:14). The writer of the book of Hebrews tells us that "the message spoken by angels was binding, and every violation and disobedience received its just punishment . . ." (2:2; see Galatians 3:19; Acts 7:53). Whether through vocal proclamation or, at times, the pens of prophets, angels as messengers delivered the true words, and thus the will of God, to humankind.

In addition, the very existence of angels as divine messengers either assumes or shows four things:

1. That truth can be transmitted from God to humanity;
2. That humankind needs to hear such truth from the Creator;
3. That spiritual error or ignorance is probably the reason such truth was conveyed; and
4. That the Creator has a personal interest in His creation.

Another word for that "personal interest" is *love*. In this way angels stand as emblems of God's love for humankind.

19

The Prophets Reveal God's Word

> "I am a fellow servant with you and with your brothers
> the prophets and of all who keep the words of this book.
> . . ." Then he told me, "Do not seal up the words of the
> prophecy of this book, because the time is near."
>
> Revelation 22:9–10

A prophet, simply put, is the mouthpiece of God. He reveals to humankind the mind of God. Since angels, too,
serve as the mouthpiece of God, might they not be considered prophets? (In fact, the goal of this book is to examine the prophetic utterances of angels.) Likewise, since
the prophet delivers messages from God, in a sense he
might be considered an angel, a "messenger." But why
blur these titles that have attained a technical distinction
with very clear referents?

Angels believe in prophets and, thus, in prophecy. No
fewer than seven times does an angel mention one or the
other to the apostle John in the book of Revelation. One

angel calls the words of what came to be known as "The Revelation of John" *prophecy:* "Do not seal up the words of the prophecy of this book . . ." (22:10). In one instance an angel actually tells John to prophesy: "Then I was told, 'You must prophesy again about many peoples, nations, languages and kings'" (10:11). Another angel tells John, in reference to the prophecies foretelling the unfolding drama of the end times, that God will use evil to destroy evil "until God's words are fulfilled" (17:17). Gabriel tells Zechariah that his angelic words of prophecy about John the Baptist "will come true at their proper time" (Luke 1:20).

Prophetic utterances that are predictive in nature will be fulfilled. If they are not, they are not the words of God and the prophet is a false prophet (see Deuteronomy 18:17–22). Even if the prophet's predictions come true, it does not guarantee that he is not a false prophet. Moses emphasized the supremacy of objective truth over metaphysical phenomena when he wrote, "If a prophet . . . appears among you and announces to you a miraculous sign or wonder, and if the sign or wonder of which he has spoken takes place, and he says, 'Let us follow other gods' (gods you have not known) 'and let us worship them,' you must not listen to the words of that prophet . . ." (Deuteronomy 13:1–3).

Evidently the function of prophecy changed somewhat with the coming of Messiah. According to the writer of the book of Hebrews, "In the past God spoke to our forefathers through the prophets at many times and in various ways, but in these last days he has spoken to us by his Son, whom he appointed heir of all things, and through whom he made the universe" (Hebrews 1:1–2). Yet Paul confirms the perpetuity of the *gift* of prophecy until the Second Coming of Christ (see Romans 12:3–8; 1 Corinthians 12:4–28; 13:8–13; Ephesians 4:11–13).

Angels place great confidence in the integrity of true prophets. At the conclusion of the book of Revelation, which happens to be the conclusion of the completed revelation of the written Word of God, an angel says to John, "These words are trustworthy and true. The Lord, the God of the spirits of the prophets, sent his angel to show his servants the things that must soon take place" (22:6). Here, trustworthy and true words are associated with the prophets, and the identity of the Lord is made known by the phrase *the God of the spirits of the prophets.* In the angel's mind the truth of the revelation and the integrity of the apostle John are foregone conclusions, for the Lord of the prophets sent an angel to reveal these things to a prophet. There could be no greater testimonial.

Part 4

"Do Not Do It!"

What Angels Believe about Angels

No one knows me better than I know myself, and I do not know anyone better than myself. Thus I could write or say more about myself than I could about God or Jesus or angels or any other human. This makes it noteworthy that the angels speak primarily about God and Jesus. On the rare occasions that they speak about themselves, it is to debase themselves and exalt the One who created them: almighty God. This, it seems, is the hallmark of a holy angel.

A fallen angel, on the other hand, debases the Creator and looks to exalt himself, redirecting the worship and adoration of humans from God to himself.

This section is pointedly brief, since unfallen angels speak of themselves rarely and briefly.

20

Angels on Angels

Not to Be Worshiped

At this I fell at his feet to worship him. But he said to me, "Do not do it! I am a fellow servant with you and with your brothers who hold to the testimony of Jesus. Worship God!"

Revelation 19:10

I, John, am the one who heard and saw these things. And when I had heard and seen them, I fell down to worship at the feet of the angel who had been showing them to me. But he said to me, "Do not do it! I am a fellow servant with you and with your brothers the prophets and of all who keep the words of this book. Worship God!"

Revelation 22:8–9

"Do not do it! . . . Do not do it!" were the jolting words to John. The angels could not have been more clear, direct or emphatic about the worship of themselves. They were aghast that they should be the objects of worship. But don't overlook the alternative the angels gave John. They did not stop with the imperative to cease and desist; they gave the corrective injunction: "Worship God! . . . Worship God!"

In a most readable and informative book on angels, Dr. David Jeremiah writes the following:

> The Ten Commandments begin with warnings about turning away from God. It's enlightening to think how heaven's angels fit in when we go back and read the first two commandments: "You shall have no other gods before me. You shall not make for yourself an idol in the form of anything in heaven above or on the earth beneath or in the waters below. You shall not bow down to them or worship them . . ." (Exodus 20:3–5). Even something as holy as an angel in heaven above is never to be turned into an idol.[23]

What do you call an angel who tries to draw attention and adoration to himself? According to Karl Barth,

> The [role] of the angel . . . has merely been to serve, to give his witness, to help. Although he is a creature, and an exemplary and perfect creature, his task as such has simply been to come and then to go again, to pass by. He would again be a lying spirit, a demon, if he were to tarry, directing attention and love and honour and even perhaps adoration to himself, causing even momentary preoccupation with himself and enticing man to enter into dealings and fellowship with himself instead of through him into dealings and fellowship with God.[24]

Angels were not made to be worshiped. (The fact that they were *made* gives that away!) They know this. Satan knows it, too.

He also knows that he can invert the design of God if he can get humans to bow at his own feet. He tried, as you recall, to persuade the Son of God to worship him. Showing Him in a vision all the kingdoms of the world, he said to Jesus,

> "All this I will give you, . . . if you will bow down and worship me." Jesus said to him, "Away from me, Satan! For it is written: 'Worship the Lord your God, and serve him only.'" Then the devil left him, and angels came and attended him.
>
> Matthew 4:9–11

In Revelation 22:9 the angel calls himself "a fellow servant." Both of these words are instructive. If he is a *servant*, he is unworthy of worship. Only the One he serves is worthy of worship. If he is a *fellow* servant, he is in at least one respect akin to humans. That is, he is of the created order—and thus, again, unworthy of worship.

Angels know very well that there is only One worthy of worship, for there is but one God. In the Bible passages above, angels cringe at the idea that humans should worship at their feet. That would be blasphemous, for angels are but created beings, and only what exists without beginning and end—that is, outside the created order—is rightly to be worshiped. And only one Being exists outside the created order: God.

The Spirit of God, addressing the mistaken idea that Jesus Himself was an angel, inspired the writer of the epistle to the Hebrews to pen these words: "The Son is the radiance of God's glory and the exact representation of his being" (1:3). Then he asks a rhetorical question that demands a negative answer:

> For to which of the angels did God ever say, "You are my Son; today I have become your Father"? . . . And again, when God brings his firstborn into the world, he says, "Let all God's angels worship him."
>
> Hebrews 1:5–6

The Spirit-inspired writer makes a clear distinction between Jesus and angels as he continues:

> In speaking of the angels he says, "He makes his angels winds, his servants flames of fire." But about the Son he says, "Your throne, O God, will last for ever and ever, and righteousness will be the scepter of your kingdom. You have loved righteousness and hated wickedness; therefore God, your God, has set you above your companions by anointing you with the oil of joy."
>
> verses 7–9

The point is clear: Jesus, being God incarnate, may be worshiped, but angels, being of the created order, are never to be worshiped. No one warns us of this more forcefully than the angels themselves: "Do not do it! . . . Worship God!" So it was that the angels pointed the shepherds to the manger that first Christmas morning (Luke 2:8–19).[25]

Part 5

Higher and Deeper

What Angels Believe about the Nature of God

Who more than angels are qualified to share with us truths about the nature of God? Angels commune with Him in a way that we do not (but shall!). They saw His creative powers at work as He made much of the material universe in their presence, just after they themselves were formed. They observed, perhaps with bewilderment (see 1 Peter 1:12), the unfolding of God's plan for humankind.

The angels experienced the perfection of the spiritual dimension in the heavenlies and the physical dimension of the material world before the entrance into both realms of ruinous sin. Then they watched as the resulting brief condition of imperfection revealed additional, glorious attributes of Creator God.

The superior intellect of the angels, their spirit nature and their firsthand experience of God have given them insights into the nature of God that humans can receive only from divine revelation. This section examines some of those angelic insights into the nature of God.

21

"In the Beginning God..."

"Fear God and give him glory.... Worship him who made the heavens, the earth, the sea and the springs of water."

Revelation 14:7

In this final book of the Bible, an angel appeals to the men and women of earth, just before time slips into eternity, to worship the Creator God. Presumably the created order—which the angel classifies as the heavens, the earth, the sea (salt water) and the springs of water (fresh water)—is, in and of itself, overwhelming evidence not only of God's existence but of His awe-fulness. "Look at the created universe," the angel is saying. It is full of wonder and mystery. How much more, then, should the Creator of it all inspire awe and worship in man?

It is impossible to describe adequately the difference between the created order and Him who stands outside that order—that is, the eternal Creator. The chasm between the two classes is too tremendous for the human mind to grasp. The task of composing such a description is made more difficult by the fact that humans, too, in a sense, are creators. We say loosely, for instance, that an artist may create a sculpture, when in fact he may only "create" a sculpture. What I mean is that men and women cannot make something from nothing. They must have the materials handed to them. They may take the atoms and molecules of clay and reshape them, but they do not actually create them.

God is not like this. He needs no one to hand Him the materials. He alone can create from nothing.

The angels witnessed God bringing the heavens and the earth into existence (see Job 38:4–7). Little wonder, then, that one of these angels would swear by this sight! The apostle John heard this angel's oath and recorded it. The angel "raised his right hand to heaven. And he swore by him who lives for ever and ever, who created the heavens and all that is in them, the earth and all that is in it, and the sea and all that is in it . . ." (Revelation 10:5–6; see Daniel 12:7). In other words, the angel swore by God's eternalness ("who lives for ever and ever") and His Creatorship ("who created the heavens . . .").

The angel swore by the one thing above which and without which nothing exists: the Creator. (Not by happenstance did the angel speak in one breath of God's Creatorship and His eternalness. It is because God is eternal that He Himself did not need a Creator for His own existence.)

Angels, it would seem, understand much better than humans the vast difference between the created and the Creator. Intentionally joining the descriptive clause *who created the heavens* with *him who lives for ever and ever,* the angel adds immeasurably to his description of God. Not only is God eternal, but He is the cause of the created order.

Based on the poetry he wrote more than two hundred years ago, Isaac Watts may have been contemplating, among other things, the vast difference between the creature and the Creator when he penned "Alas! and Did My Savior Bleed?":

> Alas! and did my Saviour bleed,
> And did my Sovereign die?
> Would He devote that sacred head
> For such a worm as I?
>
> Was it for crimes that I have done
> He groaned upon the tree?
> Amazing pity! grace unknown!
> And love beyond degree!
>
> Well might the sun in darkness hide,
> And shut his glories in,
> When Christ, the mighty Maker, died
> For man the creature's sin.
>
> But drops of grief can ne'er repay
> The debt of love I owe:
> Here, Lord, I give myself away,
> 'Tis all that I can do.

The fourth line of the first stanza has come under fire of late by more than a few presumptuous critics and has even been rewritten. The writer should apologize, they say, for comparing men to worms. I, too, believe an apology is due, but to worms, not men! After all, worms did not rebel against God. Watts was attempting to illustrate with words the mystery, the majesty, the utterly good, the aweful otherness of the Creator and His stooping to rescue the creature. Was Watts thinking that God, in so doing, is to me as I am to a worm? The comparison makes the point, although strictly speaking, in comparing creatures (men) to other creatures (worms), the gap between creature and Creator is never truly illustrated.

How do angels, apparently the greatest of the created order, address God? If humans could eavesdrop on angels speaking to God, it would be instructive! The last book of the Bible provides us with just this opportunity. Keep in mind that the angels saw God speak the heavens and the earth into existence. Here is a sample of angelic utterance addressed to God:

> "You are worthy, our Lord and God, to receive glory and honor and power, for you created all things, and by your will they were created and have their being."
>
> Revelation 4:11

So great is this attribute of Creatorship that it becomes a point of praise and worship addressed to God Himself. Nothing differentiates angels and men from God more assuredly than this: "Lord, You created all things."

"I believe in God the Father Almighty, maker of heaven and earth"

It is not surprising that the angels take the existence of God for granted. After all, they were created by God (see Psalm 148:2–5; John 1:1–3; Colossians 1:16) and experience His direct presence (see Matthew 18:10; Revelation 12:7–9). The angel Gabriel said to Zechariah, "I stand in the presence of God . . ." (Luke 1:19). Angels do not merely "believe" in God, they *know* Him.

A great host of angels appeared to the shepherds when Jesus was born, saying, "Glory to God in the highest, and on earth peace, good will toward men" (Luke 2:14, KJV). On another occasion (as I mentioned in this chapter) they acknowledged Creator God in praise:

> "You are worthy, our Lord and God, to receive glory and honor and power, for you created all things, and by your will they were created and have their being."
>
> Revelation 4:11

Again in worship, angels fall on their faces, saying:

> "We give thanks to you, Lord God Almighty, the One who is and who was, because you have taken your great power and have begun to reign."
>
> Revelation 11:17

Finally the words of an angel to the apostle John, spoken quite forcefully, it seems, imply the angel's acknowledgment of the existence of almighty God. John had fallen at the angel's feet to worship him, but the angel was quick to correct him, informing him to direct his worship not to him but to God (see Revelation 19:10).

With this article of the Apostles' Creed, each member of the triune Godhead has now received recognition: the Father, the Son (chapters 7 and 8) and the Holy Spirit (chapter 13). Thus the direct utterances of angels corroborate the object of our worship: God in three Persons, blessed Trinity.

22

Lord of the Cosmos

The angel answered me, "These are the four spirits of heaven, going out from standing in the presence of the Lord of the whole world."

Zechariah 6:5

In this passage an angel tells us that God is the Lord of the whole world. In other words, there is no place in the world you can go where God is not Lord. If you are in Asia, He is Lord. He is Lord in North America, too. From New York to Beijing, from Moscow to New Delhi, from Johannesburg to Cairo. In fact, since He is the Creator of the stars, it does not matter where you go in the universe, from the Milky Way to the farthest galaxy; the God of whom the angel spoke to Zechariah is Lord of all.

The prophet records the praise of the seraphim, the angelic creatures, who cry, "Holy, holy, holy is the Lord Almighty; the whole earth is full of his glory" (Isaiah 6:3). It is the *whole* earth that is full of His glory, not some provincial section. Every place you can name is part of the created order, and God is Creator of it all (see Revelation

10:5–6 and Nehemiah 9:6). What He has created, He is Lord over. In the angels' worship of God, as we saw in the previous chapter, they said, "You created all things, and by your will they were created and have their being" (Revelation 4:11). He who is Creator of all is by very nature the Lord of all. It is useless for other so-called gods to lay claim to any part of creation. And since this is so, there is no room for a pantheon of gods. Pluralism is a contradiction.

In Zechariah 2:13 an angel tells the prophet to say to the people, "Be still before the Lord, *all mankind . . ."* (emphasis added). The angel's understanding of the universality of the Lord and His domain is unmistakable. God reigns over *all the earth* and over *all mankind.* Another angel appears in a dream of the pagan king Nebuchadnezzar and says, "'The decision is announced by messengers, the holy ones declare the verdict, so that the living may know that the Most High is sovereign over the kingdoms of men and gives them to anyone he wishes and sets over them the lowliest of men'" (Daniel 4:17).

One of the truths the Bible is absolutely clear about is the exclusivity of God: "Listen, people of Israel! The LORD is our God. He is the only LORD" (Deuteronomy 6:4, EB). The angels have never attested to two, three, four or a thousand gods. Throughout the Bible, from the nomadic days of Abraham to the metropolitan Mediterranean days of Saint Paul, the angels bow to only One who is Lord. The idea of a plurality of gods is rejected by angels and should be rejected by humankind as well, on the basis of divine revelation as well as logic.

The angels both declare and demonstrate which God is the true and living God, the Lord of the universe. Around His throne in heaven, the angels join two other orders of angelic creatures in worship of God:

> All the angels were standing around the throne and around the elders and the four living creatures. They fell

down on their faces before the throne and worshiped God, saying:

"Amen! Praise and glory and wisdom and thanks and honor and power and strength be to our God for ever and ever. Amen!"

Revelation 7:11–12

Not only angels are rendering praise to God, but all the created order:

Then I heard every creature in heaven and on earth and under the earth and on the sea, and all that is in them, singing:

"To him who sits on the throne . . . be praise and honor and glory and power, for ever and ever!"

Revelation 5:13

One angel in the Old Testament refers to God as the "Lord of hosts" no fewer than twelve times (see Zechariah 1:12–6:15, KJV). This is a reference to God's Lordship over not just Adam's race but all heavenly beings as well. No creature in the universe untainted by sin is deaf to His bidding; such creatures everywhere are pleased to bow before His throne or stand at His command.

For those who look on God face to face—that is, the angels—there is no confusing who is God or how many Gods there are. The angels confirm what came to be known by the children of Israel as the *Shema* (from the Hebrew word for "hear"): "Hear, O Israel: The LORD our God, the LORD is one" (Deuteronomy 6:4). He is Lord "of the whole world," of "all mankind" and "Lord of hosts" for ever and ever. And because this is true, we are exhorted to resist passive devotion to God (a contradiction in terms) and exhorted to

love the LORD your God with all your heart and with all your soul and with all your strength. . . . Impress [these commandments] on your children. Talk about them when you sit at home and when you walk along the road, when you lie down and when you get up. Tie them as symbols on your hands and bind them on your foreheads. Write them on the doorframes of your houses and on your gates.

Deuteronomy 6:5, 7–9

23

The Triunity of God

The angel answered, "The Holy Spirit will come upon you, and the power of the Most High will overshadow you. So the holy one to be born will be called the Son of God."

Luke 1:35

Theologians have identified in certain New Testament passages a technical feature that has been labeled "the Trinitarian pattern." This phenomenon occurs in verses that feature a parallel listing of what have become known as the three Persons of the Godhead—a triadic form naming the Father, the Son and the Holy Spirit. The three are grouped in such a way as to imply equality and thus co-eternalness.

Such language is found in the baptismal formula of the gospel of Matthew 28:19: "Go and make disciples of all nations, baptizing them in the name [singular] of the *Father* and of the *Son* and of the *Holy Spirit* . . ." (emphasis added).

Paul's second epistle to the Corinthians also reflects this triune relationship: "May the grace of the *Lord Jesus Christ*, and the love of *God*, and the fellowship of the *Holy Spirit* be with you all" (13:14, emphasis added). First Corinthians 12:4–6 echoes the pattern: "There are different kinds of gifts, but *the same Spirit*. There are different kinds of service, but *the same Lord*. There are different kinds of working, but *the same God* works all of them in all men" (emphasis added).

This parallel grouping of Father, Son and Holy Spirit is the epitome of blasphemy if the three are not equals. In Luke 1:35 an angel declares the divine conception of the Messiah, Jesus, initiating the Trinitarian pattern that the Holy Spirit would later inspire other writers to use:

> "*The Holy Spirit*
> will come upon you, and the power of
> *the Most High*
> will overshadow you. So the holy one to be born will be
> called
> *the Son of God.*"

With these words the angel prophesies the incarnation of the Son of God and recognizes God as triune in nature: three eternal distinctions of one divine essence.

From heaven, the very abode of God, His triune nature is hinted at by the expressions of exaltation spoken by heavenly creatures known as seraphs, or seraphim. Isaiah writes: "I saw the LORD seated on a throne, high and exalted, and the train of his robe filled the temple. Above him were seraphs, each with six wings: With two wings they covered their faces, with two they covered their feet, and with two they were flying. And they were calling to one another: 'Holy, holy, holy is the LORD Almighty; the whole earth is full of his glory'" (Isaiah 6:1–3).

Centuries later the apostle John shares a similar view of the seraphs uttering a similar expression of worship: "Each of the four living creatures had six wings and was covered with eyes all around, even under his wings. Day and night they never stop saying: 'Holy, holy, holy is the Lord God Almighty, who was, and is, and is to come'" (Revelation 4:8).

"The threefold repetition of 'Holy,'" according to Herbert Lockyer, "has justly been thought to refer to the three divine persons in the Trinity. . . ."[26]

Thus the triune nature of God is hinted at by the seraphim, who are seen by Isaiah and John, and it is alluded to by the angel Gabriel, announcing to Mary the incarnation of the Son of God.

Some commentators also believe that the three angels who met with Abraham, as recounted in Genesis 18:1–15, represent an image of the Trinity:

> The narrative has them speaking together, with one voice. This collective discourse presents them as a stylized group; they are one, and speak as one, though three, prefiguring Trinitarian theology. Augustine said of this passage: "Why should we not accept that here is visibly introduced, through visible creatures, the equality of Trinity, and indeed in the three persons, one and the same substance?"[27]

In one breath the angel speaking to Mary refers to "the Holy Spirit," "the Most High" and "the Son of God." Is it any wonder that the seraphim surrounding the throne of God repeat the threefold "Holy, holy, holy"?

24

With God All Things Are Possible

"Nothing is impossible with God."

Luke 1:37

Omnipotence, the power to do all things, is one of the classical attributes of God. Since He is the Creator of everything outside of Himself that exists, a definition of God that stops short of attributing to Him all power is a definition that cannot logically stand. For God, as Creator of all that had beginning, is capable of changing creation as He desires. Since He alone stands outside creation, and since there is no created matter in existence but that which God created, and since no created thing can be greater than its creator, God always has power over all creation, which means He is all-powerful.

The old question *Can God create a rock too big for Him to lift?* ostensibly challenges the classical definition of God as omnipotent since either a positive or negative answer proves that God's power is or can be limited. But the question is illogical since it confuses the categories of the *finite* and the *infinite,* and thus should not be answered in either the negative or the positive. The *created* (for example, the rock) cannot by nature be *infinite,* nor can the *Creator* (God) by nature be *finite.* The question is as nonsensical, then, as asking someone to draw a square circle. As the nature of the circle will not allow it to be square, so the nature of God will not allow Him to be inferior to any created thing.

The angels, who have seen God face to face and viewed the majesty and magnitude of His power and presence, confirm that "nothing is impossible with God" (Luke 1:37). What the angels state in the negative, Jesus Himself later states in the positive: "With man this is impossible, but with God all things are possible" (Matthew 19:26). In the Old Testament, the angel of the Lord asks Abraham the rhetorical question, "Is anything too hard for the Lord?" (Genesis 18:14).

In their respective contexts, the angels' utterances address the pregnancy of Mary's once barren cousin Elizabeth and the barrenness of Abraham's wife Sarah. They also speak to God's willingness to enter the physical world of humankind's earthly needs. Jesus' statement, on the other hand, addresses the seeming impossibility of humankind to enter heaven, the abode of God. He is saying, in effect, "You can't make it happen, but I can." And so He has.

25

Worthy Is the Lord

"He will command his angels concerning you, and they will lift you up in their hands, so that you will not strike your foot against a stone."

Matthew 4:6

You have come to Mount Zion, to the heavenly Jerusalem, the city of the living God. You have come to thousands upon thousands of angels in joyful assembly.

Hebrews 12:22

These passages reflect angelic responses to two distinct ways God is worthy. He is worthy of obedience, so that the angels "do his bidding," and He is worthy of praise and worship, so that the angels gather "in joyful assembly."

Let's look at each of these in turn.

Worthy of Obedience

"When we cried out to the LORD, he heard our cry and sent an angel."

Numbers 20:16

Praise the LORD, you his angels, you mighty ones who do his bidding, who obey his word.

Psalm 103:20

In this world we obey laws, orders and directives for a number of reasons, including fear of punishment, monetary gain and learned respect for authority. In the above verses it is evident that God directs angels, even to the point that they interact with humans and change the course of human history! He sends them; they do His bidding. But why do angels obey?

Although the holy angels are in a state of perfection, still they are aware of the unfathomable chasm between Creator God and themselves. And they obey not because of the splendor of what He has produced, but because of the sublimeness of who He is. The very supremacy and majesty of His being commands obedience. According to Barth,

> They do exactly, neither more nor less nor other than, what God wills. . . . And in their way they do it exactly as He wills it to be done. What distinguishes their doing of it from that of other obedient creatures is that in it there is no question of creaturely autonomy. The possibility of deviation or omission does not arise. Their obedience does not have to come into being, and it has no limit. Their creaturely freedom is identical with their obedience.[28]

Jesus commented that humans in heaven "will be like the angels" in regard to marriage (Matthew 22:30; Mark

12:25). It seems to me that we may be like angels in more than just this regard. I believe that our will to obey, even as the will of angels, will be transformed into a freedom to obey to the utmost. Even to say we will have absolute freedom to resist disobedience does not express it strongly enough. As radical as the shift will be from earth to heaven, so will be our changing natures. In the presence of God we will not even consider disobedience.

Worthy of Praise and Worship

"Where were you when I laid the earth's foundation?
　　Tell me, if you understand.
Who marked off its dimensions? Surely you know!
　　Who stretched a measuring line across it?
On what were its footings set,
　　or who laid its cornerstone—
while the morning stars sang together
　　and all the angels shouted for joy?"

Job 38:4–7

The angelic worship of God of which this passage speaks is not reserved, somber, cringing, liturgical or contemplative. It is excited, exuberant, exhilarating and ecstatic: "All the angels shouted for joy." Line this up with the scene of "thousands upon thousands of angels in joyful assembly" (Hebrews 12:22).

Although we have discussed some of the following verses earlier in the book, we have not examined these awe-inspiring utterances as actual words of angelic worship:

I looked and heard the voice of many angels, numbering thousands upon thousands, and ten thousand times ten thousand. They encircled the throne and the living creatures and the elders. In a loud voice they sang:

> "Worthy is the Lamb, who was slain, to receive power
> and wealth and wisdom and strength and honor and glory
> and praise!"
>
> ... All the angels were standing around the throne and
> around the elders and the four living creatures. They fell
> down on their faces before the throne and worshiped God,
> saying:
>
> "Amen! Praise and glory and wisdom and thanks and
> honor and power and strength be to our God for ever and
> ever. Amen!"
>
> Revelation 5:11–12; 7:11–12

No other book of the Bible reveals the majesty and awe-
someness of God as powerfully as the book of Revelation.
One reason for this is that no other book deals as exten-
sively with angels, who see and worship God face to face.
(The word for *angel* is found 184 times in the New Testament; 79 of those occurrences, or 43 percent, are found
in the book of Revelation. For this reason Revelation has
been called the "angel book" of the New Testament.) Here
the secrets of the courts of heaven are glimpsed, and the
future of the children of God is hinted at when we, too,
can experience the presence of God face to face.

In Revelation 5:13–14 we find humans joining in angelic praise. In fact, the entire created order acknowledges
the God of all creation and lifts voices of praise to Him:

> Then I heard every creature in heaven and on earth and
> under the earth and on the sea, and all that is in them,
> singing:
>
> "To him who sits on the throne and to the Lamb be
> praise and honor and glory and power, for ever and ever!"
>
> The four living creatures said, "Amen," and the elders
> fell down and worshiped.

In the churches of the Western world where we take
pride in the democratic political process and our egalitar-

ian culture, we no longer give much thought to bowing to royalty. In the world to come, however, that will change! We will want to fall on our faces before our sovereign Lord, and it will be up to God whether we ever again desire to stand.

26

God Cares

"The Lord has heard of your misery."

Genesis 16:11

"God will wipe away every tear from their eyes."

Revelation 7:17

A survey of the world's religions reveals only two from which God emerges as loving, caring and personal—Judaism and Christianity. Many would consider these as one religion, Judaism being the rich beginning of Christianity and Christianity being the glorious culmination and prophetic fulfillment of Judaism.[29]

In Genesis 16:11 we find an angel of the Lord telling Hagar, whom Abraham had used wrongly in his attempt to bring about God's promise of a multitude of descendants, "You are now with child and you will have a son. You shall name him Ishmael [Hebrew for *God hears*], for the Lord has heard of your misery." Hagar was not the one God had in mind to give birth to the nation of Israel and continue the lineage from which would come the Messiah. He did not abandon Hagar in her misery, however, but made her a promise just as binding as His promise to Abraham (see Genesis 12:1–3).

Later, when Abraham had abandoned Hagar and her son in the desert of Beersheba and they were on the threshold of death,

> God heard the boy crying, and the angel of God called to Hagar from heaven and said to her, "What is the matter, Hagar? Do not be afraid; God has heard the boy crying as he lies there. Lift the boy up and take him by the hand, for I will make him into a great nation."
>
> Genesis 21:17–18

Two lines stand out in these two passages from Genesis: "The Lord has heard of your misery" and "God has heard the boy crying." If ever humans need to feel the presence of God, it is during the times of the dark night of the soul. There is no reason to think God has ever abandoned us, that He does not know our misery or does not hear our cries. Surely He has gauged the very warmth and wetness of our tears and stands ready to work all things for our good (see Romans 8:28). "The intervention of the angel on Hagar's journeys," writes Judith Lang, "reveals the all-seeing and purposeful compassion of God."[30]

The greatest of fallen angels, Satan, unwittingly testifies to God's protection and blessing of His people. The book of Job records his complaint: "Have you not put a hedge around [Job] and his household and everything he has? You have blessed the work of his hands, so that his flocks and herds are spread throughout the land" (1:10). Perhaps we should remind Satan of his own words when we are in dire need of God's protection and provision. Just say, "Satan, you know God has put a hedge around me and mine and is blessing my work. You admitted as much when you said it of Job."

Unseen Emissaries of Mercy

One night almost two thousand years ago, a ship was being tossed by a tremendous storm. On board that ship was, among many others, the evangelist Paul. He had made an appeal to Caesar for charges brought against him and was being transported with other prisoners from Caesarea to Rome. The night before the storm an angel appeared to him and said, "Do not be afraid, Paul. You must stand trial before Caesar; and God has graciously given you the lives of all who sail with you" (Acts 27:24). This Spirit-inspired story, memorialized in the Acts of the Apostles, stands as an encouragement to all of us as we endure life's storms.

Several years ago a popular song recorded these words: "Angels watching over me, everywhere I go. . . ." The song went on to talk about the help we receive unknowingly from unseen angels. In the routine of life it is easy to disbelieve or forget their presence. But passages in the Old Testament indicate they can operate invisibly if they wish.

Recall the prophet Balaam traveling on his donkey when the animal stopped suddenly. An angel standing in the path was made manifest to the donkey, but Balaam did not see him until the Lord opened his eyes. The angel said to Balaam, "I have come here to oppose you because your path is a reckless one before me" (Numbers 22:32). Balaam was about to step out of the will of God and injure the children of Israel, but God sent this angel to stop him.

Perhaps something similar occurs a million times a day and we do not even know it. But because God cares for us and loves us, He, in His perfect plan and timing, both permits and prevents our steps and the steps of those who oppose us.

In 2 Kings 6 a defending host of angels surrounded Elisha and his servant, but the servant could see only the enemies who encircled the city of Dothan. The frightened servant had to be calmed by Elisha:

> "Don't be afraid. . . . Those who are with us are more than those who are with them." And Elisha prayed, "O LORD, open his eyes so he may see." Then the LORD opened the servant's eyes, and he looked and saw the hills full of horses and chariots of fire all around Elisha.
>
> verses 16–17

Herbert Lockyer comments on this passage:

> We, too, need the inner conviction regarding the invisible armies commissioned to guard God's servants when they are most exposed to danger. Elisha saw the mountains full of horses and chariots of fire—his servant saw only the Syrians, until the Lord opened his eyes.[31]

In the New Testament an angel served as a divine guardian over the Messiah, rescuing Him from King Herod's slaughter of innocents in Bethlehem:

> An angel of the Lord appeared to Joseph in a dream. "Get up," he said, "take the child and his mother and escape to Egypt. Stay there until I tell you, for Herod is going to search for the child to kill him." So he got up, took the child and his mother during the night and left for Egypt, where he stayed until the death of Herod.
>
> Matthew 2:13–15

Jesus, as an adult, would be ministered to by angels during the severe trials of His life—once after His temptation in the desert and again in Gethsemane, the night before His crucifixion (see Matthew 4:11; Luke 22:43–44).

If God Cares, Why Do I Hurt?

God is often blamed—wrongly, I believe—for the pain and suffering in the world today (which, by the way, He, too, experienced through the incarnation). And another protest is raised by many: If there is a God, why doesn't He put an end to the pain and suffering on earth?

The answer is, *He is!* The apostle John recorded in the book of Revelation the words of an angelic creature whose abode was around the throne of God. The angel, speaking of believers who had passed through the great Tribulation and were now entering the presence of God, said, "God will wipe away every tear from their eyes" (7:17). The majestic plan of God is unfolding in the heavenlies and on the earth. The God who hears our cries and who knows our misery, even firsthand, offers to all humankind abundant life in an eternal state where the angels reiterate that "he will wipe every tear from their eyes. There will be no more death or mourning or crying or pain" (Revelation 21:4). This new world, absent of pain, is so radically different that the angel describes the change by saying that "the old order of things has passed away."

God is not powerless to put an end to pain; neither is He powerless to use it for good (while granting our free will). For now He chooses to use it for good, though the good of much of it is lost on His fleshly, finite creatures. But the time will come when He will put an end to it. Until then it may remain mysterious and inscrutable.

Is it possible that much of eternity will be spent enjoying the unveiling of this mystery of pain? Perhaps then pain will turn into joy, and great pain into great joy, and we will understand all the more the depth of God's love and the extent of His care (see John 9:1–3; Romans 8:18; Hebrews 10:32–36). Along these lines Judith Lang writes:

> The apocalyptic visions in the Bible . . . reveal angels at work in bringing about the final triumph of God over all evil. The universe and all it contains will be brought through evil into ultimate good. This is the "order" that the angels are keeping. Satan's disordered angelic nature, on the other hand, could be set on introducing disorder, or evil, wherever possible, in vain attempts to slow down or pervert the progress of God's purpose. But because the Devil is confined to what is passing away, he has no possibility of destroying the words of Christ, who has "the words of eternal life" (John 6:68). . . .
>
> Suffering is built into human existence, but every grief has the potential to pass into ultimate life. Pain is endured by the whole human race in solidarity, and in that there can be a flame of resurrection hope.[32]

27

God of Justice, God of Mercy

With the coming of dawn, the angels urged Lot, saying, "Hurry! Take your wife and your two daughters who are here, or you will be swept away when the city is punished." When he hesitated, the men [angels] grasped his hand and the hands of his wife and of his two daughters and led them safely out of the city, for the LORD was merciful to them.

Genesis 19:15–16

The destruction of Sodom and Gomorrah, according to the angels, was not arbitrary. God had a reason for dissolving the charters of these cities: *wickedness*. The angels declared to Lot that the city was going to be punished. The context makes it clear that the punishment was the result of the evil manifested in the citizens of the city.

The words of the angels confirm that it is not in God's nature to accept uncritically all actions to which man's imagination gives rise. Our God rejects behavior that is substandard, His own nature defining the standard; while He accepts all that conforms to His nature. The former we consider evil, the latter good. The basis of the distinction is not something outside of God, making Him subject to it. It lies in the nature of God Himself. His own majestic holiness creates the touchstone.

In the midst of the punishment of Sodom and Gomorrah, some were spared. The same angels who came to destroy the cities (see Genesis 19:13) came to rescue Abraham's nephew.[33] The Bible says that the angels actually grabbed the hands of Lot, his wife and their two daughters and led them to safety outside the doomed cities. Because the angels were acting as God's agents, Moses recounts that, through the action of the angels, "the Lord was merciful to them" (verse 16).

This story demonstrates two important scriptural principles. On the one hand, God destroys; on the other, He rescues. The justice of God is reflected in the punishment of Sodom and Gomorrah, whereas the mercy of God is reflected in the preservation of Lot and his family. Herbert Lockyer observes these twin principles when he writes that "while [the angels] were messengers of mercy on behalf of Lot and his two daughters, they were also ministers of vengeance, for were they not sent by God to witness the guilt of Sodom and punish it?"[34]

Since Lot and his family were sinners, too (see Romans 3:23), why save them? As the nephew of Abraham, Lot apparently came under the protective covenant: "Thus it was that, when God destroyed the cities of the plain, he did not forget Abraham and he rescued Lot from the midst of the overthrow, when he overthrew the cities where Lot was living" (Genesis 19:29, NJB).

No doubt this benevolence found its basis in God's unmerited grace and was reflected in Lot's own similitude to the touchstone. Peter writes that Lot was "a righteous man, who was distressed by the filthy lives of lawless men" (2 Peter 2:7).

Part 6

Book's Ending, Life's Beginning

What an Angel Told Others to Tell You

From the creation of the world to its consummation, angels have been witnesses and, often, integral players in earthly affairs. From the splendor of earth's creation and re-creation to the mundane task of guarding a man's or woman's footsteps, myriad angelic beings have been and continue to be busy on the earth.

In some mysterious way angels have been involved in delivering the prayers of humans to God and the answers to those prayers from God to humans. More important, they have delivered to humankind the revelation of God's Son. His coming was prophesied by an angel and recounted in the Hebrew Scriptures, and the same angel announced the fulfillment of that prophecy five centuries later, recorded in the Greek Scriptures. Thus, angels have revealed to humankind the very love of God.

I leave you with most important words from the lips of an angel.

28

"This New Life ..."

"Angel messages are more than just bits and pieces of divine information dropped like propaganda leaflets from heavenly aviators," writes Gary Kinnaman. "Angel messages pulsate with the presence of the Lord. Angels are beings of light and their messages glow with God."[35] Because this is so, our attention to the messages of the angels is of eternal importance.

In the preceding pages we have seen that angels confirm every essential Christian doctrine. (They confirm other, less important doctrines, too. I will leave these for you to ferret out and savor.) You might be wondering, "What is the greatest truth the angels teach us?" Without a doubt it is this: *God loves us and wants to have a loving, eternal relationship with us.*

The fact that you are reading this book about angels says something about your interests. It probably says you want to know more about God. You might even be searching for Him. I must ask you this question: *Are you prepared for what you may find?*

Early one Jerusalem morning almost two thousand years ago, two distraught female believers went to the tomb of Jesus, desiring to dress the body of their revered and respected Teacher with spices and perfumes. When they arrived they were startled by the empty tomb and an angel, who said to them, "Do not be afraid, for I know that you are looking for Jesus . . ." (Matthew 28:5).

Perhaps you, too, in your way, have been searching for God and are startled to discover that all along you have been looking for Jesus. I believe the words of the angel are appropriate for you, too: "Do not be afraid." You need not fear because He is who He said He was and because "he has risen, just as he said" (Matthew 28:6). The eternal, abundant life He promised believers was validated and sealed by His resurrection, in which He invites all of us to share. This is the new life spoken about by an angel, who told Jesus' disciples, "Go, stand in the temple courts . . . and tell the people the full message of this new life" (Acts 5:20). In the verses that follow that text, we learn that "the full message of this new life" includes, for the believer, the forgiveness of sins through the crucifixion and resurrection of Jesus and the gift of the Holy Spirit (see Acts 5:29–32).

Are you interested in the "new life" spoken of by the angel? God offers this new and eternal life to you. Because it is new and abundant, you can experience it joyously here and now, even though you may be in the midst of external violence and turmoil or interior agony and despair. And because it is eternal, you will experience it with God forever.

Since God has already done the work, all you have to do is accept His loving reach, as He has stretched out both arms for you.

Appendix

Why Believe the Bible
or Angels at All?

There are thousands of stories about angels, some from the Bible, some not. Why believe any of them?

It is a good question, but I have not set out in this book to prove the existence of angels, or even the possibility of their existence.[36] Rather I have presupposed that they exist. I have also assumed the authenticity and reliability of the best source about angels: the holy Scriptures.

It seems unfair, however, to try to bring readers with no knowledge of the trustworthiness of the Bible to an appreciation of angelic utterances that come from the Bible. If the primary source of evidence about angels lacks credibility, there is much room for doubt, skepticism or outright disbelief.

For this reason I would like to use the remaining pages to review some of the evidence that supports the reliability of the Bible.[37]

The Manuscript Evidence

The Bible was written over a period of fifteen hundred years, from 1400 B.C. to A.D. 100, by forty or so authors. The Old Testament was written primarily in the Hebrew language and the New Testament in Greek. Until A.D. 1455 every Bible was hand-copied, which raises an important question: How reliable are copies of copies of copies? After all, most of us have played the game of "Gossip" in which someone whispers something to one person, who must whisper it to another, until the message has gone around the room. Usually the final words bear comically little resemblance to the initial utterance.

So how do we know the words in the Bible are anywhere close to what was originally written? How careful were the copyists?

The Old Testament

According to Old Testament scholar Samuel Davidson, the following was the process that one ancient school of Old Testament copyists observed:

[1] A synagogue roll must be written on the skins of clean animals, [2] prepared for the particular use of the synagogue by a Jew. [3] These must be fastened together with strings taken from clean animals. [4] Every skin must contain a certain number of columns, equal throughout the entire codex. [5] The length of each column must not extend over less than 48 or more than 60 lines; and the breadth must consist of thirty letters. [6] The whole copy must be first-lined; and if three words be written without a line, it is worthless. [7] The ink should be black, neither red, green, nor any other colour, and be prepared according to a definite recipe. [8] An authentic copy must be the exemplar, from which the transcriber ought not in the least deviate. [9] No word or letter, not even a *yod*, must be writ-

ten from memory, the scribe not having looked at the codex before him . . . ; [10] Between every consonant the space of a hair or thread must intervene; [11] between every new *parashah,* or section, the breadth of nine consonants; [12] between every book, three lines. [13] The fifth book of Moses must terminate exactly with a line; but the rest need not do so. [14] Besides this, the copyist must sit in full Jewish dress, [15] wash his whole body, [16] not begin to write the name of God with a pen newly dipped in ink, [17] and should a king address him while writing that name he must take no notice of him.[38]

Later the Masoretes (Jewish scribes) selectively appointed copyists who painstakingly protected the integrity of the text. They handled it, according to F. F. Bruce,

with the greatest imaginable reverence, and devised a complicated system of safeguards against scribal slips. They counted, for example, the number of times each letter of the alphabet occurs in each book; they pointed out the middle letter of the Pentateuch and the middle letter of the whole Hebrew Bible, and made even more detailed calculations than these. "Everything countable seems to be counted," says Wheeler Robinson . . . and they made up mnemonics by which the various totals might be readily remembered.[39]

The real test of the copying process came in 1947 with the discovery of the Dead Sea Scrolls, which included the book of Isaiah. Until then the earliest Old Testament manuscript dated from A.D. 900. The Dead Sea Isaiah scroll dated from circa 125 B.C.—that is, one thousand years earlier than the oldest extant manuscript. A comparison of the two texts would test the skill and care of the copyists. Here is what it revealed:

Of the 177 words in Isaiah 53, there are only seventeen letters in question. Ten of these letters are simply a matter of spelling, which does not affect the sense. Four more letters are minor stylistic changes, such as conjunctions. The remaining three letters comprise the word "light," which is added in verse 11, and does not affect the meaning greatly. Furthermore, this word is supported by the LXX [Septuagint] and IQ Is[b]. Thus, in one chapter of 166 words, there is only one word (three letters) in question after a thousand years of transmission—and this word does not significantly change the meaning of the passage.[40]

There is no reason to believe, given this evidence, that the Old Testament was corrupted by the continuous copying. Rather, it was preserved with an astonishing degree of faithfulness.

The New Testament

The evidence for the trustworthiness of the New Testament is likewise formidable, although the proof is of a different kind. The credibility of the New Testament is found in the eyewitness accounts, the proximity of the writings to the events, the age and quantity of extant manuscripts, and collateral witnesses.

The four gospels were written by eyewitnesses or contemporaries of Jesus. They relate the events in Jesus' life and teachings and have been dated between A.D. 45 and 90. (Their source documents would have been around for some time before that.)[41] Some epistles of Paul date to within eighteen years of the crucifixion. James, the half-brother of Jesus, wrote his epistle within seventeen years of the crucifixion.

The oldest existing fragment of the New Testament is known as the John Ryland Fragment, which is dated A.D. 117–130. It was found not in Asia Minor, where the original is believed to have been penned, but in the sands of Egypt. Thus, when time is allowed for further copying and transport, this papyrus fragment pushes the date of the gospel of John back to the century of the events described. The Chester Beatty Papyri are dated A.D. 200 and contain major portions of the New Testament. As early as A.D. 160, Tatian, an early Church father, created the *Diatessaron*, a harmony of the four gospels.

There exist more than five thousand Greek manuscripts containing all or parts of the New Testament. In addition there are nine thousand early translations into the Latin, Syriac and Coptic languages. With this multitude of manuscript evidence, scholars have been able to reconstruct the original words of the New Testament to an accuracy of 99 percent or better. The remaining one percent is made up of inconsequential variants.

In addition to manuscript evidence, there is the witness of the early Church fathers, some of whom lived in the same century as Jesus. They include Clement of Rome (A.D. 95), Ignatius (A.D. 70–110), Polycarp (A.D. 70–156), Tatian (A.D. 170), Irenaeus (A.D. 170), Justin Martyr (A.D. 133), Clement of Alexandria (A.D. 150–212), Origen (A.D. 185–253), Tertullian (A.D. 160–220) and others. The writings of these men, according to J. Harold Greenlee, are so chock full of Scripture quotations that the New Testament "could virtually be reconstructed from them without the use of New Testament manuscripts."[42] Sir David Dalrymple set out to search the early fathers for every New Testament verse. He found all but eleven.[43]

How does this manuscript evidence compare to secular works whose authenticity is unquestioned? Plato wrote in 400 B.C.; only seven copies exist, the earliest dates around A.D. 900. Caesar's *Gallic Wars* was written around 100–44 B.C.; there are only ten extant copies and the earliest dates around A.D. 900. Tacitus wrote his *Annals* around A.D. 100; twenty copies exist and the earliest dates to around A.D. 1100. For all these ancient works, the time gap between the age of the earliest copy and the date of the original is more than one thousand years.

The extant New Testament manuscripts, by contrast, number 5,366; the earliest dates to around A.D. 114, leaving a gap of only fifty years between the age of the copy and the date of the original.[44] In assessing the disparity of New Testament manuscript evidence with that of other ancient works, John Warwick Montgomery writes that "to be skeptical of the resultant text of the New Testament books is to allow all of classical antiquity to slip into obscurity, for no documents of the ancient period are as well attested bibliographically as the New Testament."[45]

The manuscript evidence for the New Testament is early, it exists in great quantity and it is supported by the collateral witness of men who lived in the first and second centuries. Scholars have judged the New Testament to be "99.9 percent free of significant variants."[46] Thus there is no reason to believe that the New Testament we have today differs in substance from the original written in the first century. The transmission of God's divine revelation to humanity was, by the account of the manuscript evidence, successful.

The Evidence of Fulfilled Prophecies

Although it is necessary to have a trustworthy copy of God's written revelation, reconstructing the original words of a document does not prove that the document is, in fact, inspired by God. How do we get to that point? One way, I believe, is to show that the document contains predictive prophecies beyond the pale of human knowledge and coincidence.

Peter W. Stoner, former chairman of the Departments of Mathematics and Astronomy of Pasadena City College, applied the laws of probability to eleven Old Testament prophecies and concluded that "the probability of these eleven prophecies coming true, if written in human wisdom, is . . . 1 in 5.76 x 10^{59}."[47]

Stoner also applied the principles of probability to eight messianic prophecies of the Old Testament that were fulfilled in Jesus as revealed in the New Testament. The eight prophetic predictions, he concluded, had only one chance in 10^{17} of being fulfilled in one man. Stoner used the following illustration to show the probability of this happening:

> Suppose that we take 10^{17} silver dollars and lay them on the face of Texas. They will cover all of the state two feet deep. Now mark one of these silver dollars and stir the whole mass thoroughly, all over the state. Blindfold a man and tell him that he can travel as far as he wishes, but he must pick up one silver dollar and say that this is the right one. What chance would he have of getting the right one? Just the same chance that the prophets would have had of writing these eight prophecies and having them all come true in any one man, from their day to the present, providing they wrote them in their own wisdom.[48]

But there are more than eight messianic prophecies fulfilled in Christ. Stoner went on to calculate the chances of any one man's fulfilling 48 prophecies to be 1 in 10^{157}.

The following illustration from *The Case for Jesus the Messiah* shows just how large this number is:

> Imagine one ant traveling at the speed of only *one inch* every 15 billion years. If he could only carry one atom at a time, how many atoms could he move in 10^{157} years? He could, even at that incredibly slow speed, be able to move all the atoms in 600,000 trillion, trillion, trillion universes the size of our universe, a distance of 30 billion light years![49]

This illustrates the fulfilling of 48 messianic prophecies, but there are as many as 456! This proof must be reckoned with by anyone who chooses to deny the supernatural character of the Bible.

The Evidence of the Church

That the Church even exists points to the reliability of the Scriptures. For one thing, the existence of the Church cannot be disputed. Obviously it is here now; indisputably it has not always existed. Historical and archeological evidence for the Church indicates that it emerged onto the scene in first-century Palestine. In 1945 a burial chamber in Jerusalem yielded two inscriptions on ossuaries, or caskets. These inscriptions are prayers to Jesus and date to between A.D. 40 and 50.[50] No sufficient impetus for the Church's origin and growth, other than the New Testament account, has ever been proven.

The Church arose as a persecuted minority Jewish sect. All twelve of its founding apostles were persecuted, and all but one were martyred for their faith. Hundreds of other followers chose martyrdom rather than deny their faith in the resurrected Jesus. As for the obvious rebuttal that many people have died for mistaken beliefs, McDowell and Wilson have made this reply in reference to the eleven disciples:

> Yes, a lot of people have died for a lie, but they thought it was the truth. Now if the resurrection didn't take place (i.e., was false), the disciples knew it. I find no way to demonstrate that they could have been deceived. Therefore these eleven men not only died for a lie—here is the catch—but they knew it was a lie. It would be hard to find eleven people in history who died for a lie, knowing it was a lie.[51]

To say that the New Testament documents were mistaken or false means that the early martyrs chose to die for what they knew was untrue. The picture the gospels draw of the post-crucifixion disciples as a frightened, cowardly little huddle hardly looks like a group of men who would challenge the formidable power of the Jewish authorities, much less the unmatched might of the Roman Empire. Furthermore, to suggest that the disciples lied about Jesus goes head-on against the moral teachings of the Savior.

So are we to believe that the disciples held the moral teachings of Jesus so highly that they lied about His resurrection? It does not stand to reason. Their very purpose in following Jesus would prevent them from fabricating such an outrageous story about Him. This strengthens the conclusion that their accounts of Jesus' words and deeds as recorded in the New Testament are true.

The Evidence of Changed Lives

One of the two remaining evidences has, more than anything else, changed the shape of our world. It is the evidence of people whose lives were transformed by the power of the Gospel.

There exists within each human a component of being that biblical writers refer to as the spirit or soul.[52] It (though perhaps not it alone) is what sets humans apart from animals. The soul is the nonmaterial, eternal component of each human being. Since it is viewed as the core of human personality and the seat of human emotions, it is viewed spatially as an interior component. Thus it is often viewed figuratively as "the heart."

The heart is the human component that can be in a communicative relationship with the numinous. When we reach out to God or actually hear His voice, we do so through our spirits. Saint Augustine referred to this longing of the soul when he said, "Thou madest us for Thyself, and our heart is restless, until it repose in Thee."[53] Another writer, perhaps Blaise Pascal, the seventeenth-century mathematician, physicist and philosopher, expressed a similar sentiment when he said that within the heart of every man is a God-shaped vacuum.

The condition of the soul affects the attitude and behavior of the individual. If this were not so, personal spiritual renewal or regeneration would be imperceptible to those around us. But attitude and behavior changes are usually apparent in someone who has had such a religious experience. Christian history is full of individuals who have made 180-degree turns in their lives. Don't take my word for it. Ask any Christian. Many have had such a life-changing experience. Prostitutes have become virtuous; thieves have stopped stealing; the greedy have become generous; the chemically dependent have been freed from addictions; adulterers and homosexuals have become chaste; murderers have melted in repentance and become lovers of human life.[54]

The list goes on, but I think you get the point. The Gospel, the good news of Jesus' death and resurrection on behalf of sinful men and women, has the power to transform the soul, which is exactly what the Bible claims.

The Evidence of the Greatest Ethic

The final evidence we will look at that supports the reliability of the Bible is the evidence of the Gospel itself, which has the capacity more than anything else to change the world for the better. I am not aware of the teachings of any greater ethic than Jesus' ethic of love. If it were applied by every individual alive, we would live in the long-imagined utopia. You might even say we would be in heaven!

Here are some of Jesus' teachings on love:

1. "Love the Lord your God with all your heart and with all your soul and with all your mind. This is the first and greatest commandment. And the second is like it: Love your neighbor as yourself" (Matthew 22:37–39).
2. "Greater love has no one than this, that he lay down his life for his friends" (John 15:13). (Quite a contrast to the words of one fallen angel: "A man will give all he has for his own life" [Job 2:4].)
3. "This is my command: Love each other" (John 15:17).
4. "Do to others as you would have them do to you" (Luke 6:31).
5. "Give to the one who asks you, and do not turn away from the one who wants to borrow from you" (Matthew 5:42).

But Jesus did not stop here. He extended His ethic of love to include even those who did not show love in return.

6. "Do not resist an evil person. If someone strikes you on the right cheek, turn to him the other also" (Matthew 5:39).
7. "You have heard that it was said, 'Love your neighbor and hate your enemy.' But I tell you: Love your enemies and pray for those who persecute you" (Matthew 5:43–44).

Oh, to live in a world where such teachings were practiced! This is the ethic of the Bible, whether or not it is practiced by all or any who call themselves Christians; and the truth of this teaching resonates within the heart of every human being. You might call this a *numinous* verification of the trustworthiness of the holy Scriptures.

So strong is this ethic that some have argued that even if there were no God, and thus no good, to follow the ethic would still be admirable. Simone Weil writes,

145

If we put obedience to God above everything else, unreservedly, with the following thought: "Suppose God is real, then our gain is total—even though we fall into nothingness at the moment of death; suppose the word 'God' stands only for illusions, then we have still lost nothing because on this assumption there is absolutely nothing good, and consequently nothing to lose; we have even gained . . . because we have left aside the illusory goods which exist but are not good for the sake of something which (on this assumption) does not exist but which if it did exist, would be the only good. . . ."

If one follows this rule of life, then no revelation at the moment of death can cause any regrets; because if chance or the devil govern all worlds we would still have no regrets for having lived this way.[55]

In a world of war, cruelty and barbarism, in cultures that knew nothing but death, decimation and destruction, where might made right and the weak were doomed, there emerged from an obscure corner of the world, out of the mouth of a Jewish carpenter, a new paradigm: Love your enemies, go the extra mile, turn the other cheek. How could a paradigm of peace, humility and self-sacrifice overtake the age-old paradigm of brute force? Can a rabbit chase a lion from his den? There is no power in self-sacrifice unless it is followed by resurrection. This became the power that no army could match, no tyrant defeat and no entrenched paradigm suppress.

To sum up, the evidence for the trustworthiness of the Bible includes:

1. The reliability of the copying process;
2. The proximity of the writers and their writings to the events described;
3. The age of the extant manuscripts;
4. The quantity of early manuscripts;

5. The fulfilled prophecies in the Old and New Testaments;
6. The origin and explosive growth of the early Church;
7. The motivation for martyrdom of Christians who were contemporaries of Jesus;
8. The unlikelihood of the early Christians adhering to the moral teachings of Jesus and at the same time propagating a distortion of Him;
9. The lives of those changed by the power of the Gospel;
10. The power of Jesus' ethic of love to transform the world.

For the foregoing reasons I accept the reliability, authenticity and truth of the Bible. And thus I can trust what the angels of Scripture have said to humankind.

Notes

1. Karl Barth, *Church Dogmatics: The Doctrine of Creation,* Vol. 3, Pt. 3, trans. by G. W. Bromiley and R. J. Ehrlich (Edinburgh: T & T Clark, 1960), pp. 451–452.

2. Ibid., p. 463.

3. Ibid., pp. 483–484.

4. Quoted in Herbert Lockyer, *All the Angels in the Bible* (Peabody, Mass.: Hendrickson, 1995), p. 167.

5. David Jeremiah, *What the Bible Says about Angels: Powerful Guardians, a Mysterious Presence, God's Messengers* (Sisters, Ore.: Multnomah, 1996), pp. 57–58.

6. Quoted in Lockyer, p. 4.

7. Ibid., p. 10.

8. Barth, *Dogmatics,* p. 460.

9. I have omitted the clause *He descended into hell [or hades]* because it is a much later addition to the Creed; see Wayne Grudem, *Systematic Theology: An Introduction to Biblical Doctrine* (Grand Rapids: Zondervan, 1994), pp. 586–594.

10. John Calvin, trans. by Ford Lewis Battles, ed. by John T. McNeill, *Institutes of the Christian Religion* (Philadelphia: Westminster, 1960), p. 503.

11. Ron Rhodes, *Angels among Us* (Eugene, Ore.: Harvest House, 1994), pp. 147–148.

12. Judith Lang, *The Angels of God: Understanding the Bible* (London: New City Press, 1997), p. 132.

13. Barth, *Dogmatics,* p. 440.

14. Robert H. Mounce, "The Book of Revelation," *The New International Commentary on the New Testament* (Grand Rapids: Eerdmans, 1977), p. 148.

15. A detailed explication of Daniel 9:24–26 may be found in Moishe Rosen's *Y'shua* (Chicago: Moody, 1982), pp. 37–40, and in John Ankerberg's *Case for Jesus the Messiah* (Eugene, Ore.: Harvest House, 1995), pp. 67–73. These works

also discuss many of the more than four hundred Old Testament prophetic, messianic references to Christ.

16. This is not to say that the resurrection body is unchanged or in every way identical to the earthly body. It is a glorified body, possibly acclimated to new dimensions, for after His resurrection Jesus consumed food (see Luke 24:41–43) and invited others to touch Him (John 20:27), yet seemed to materialize and dematerialize (see Luke 24:31; John 20:19, 26).

17. Barth, *Dogmatics,* pp. 439–440.

18. Duane A. Garrett, *Angels and the New Spirituality* (Nashville: Broadman & Holman, 1995), p. 31.

19. Ibid., p. 51.

20. Ibid., p. 57.

21. James W. Sire, *Why Should Anyone Believe Anything at All?* (Downers Grove, Ill.: InterVarsity, 1994), p. 183.

22. Lang, *Angels,* p. 100.

23. Jeremiah, *Angels,* p. 53.

24. Barth, *Dogmatics,* p. 481.

25. Ibid., p. 505.

26. Lockyer, *Angels,* p. 32.

27. Lang, *Angels,* p. 107.

28. Barth, *Dogmatics,* p. 493; see Thomas Aquinas, *Summa Theologica,* trans. by the Fathers of the English Dominican Province, Part 1, 62, 8 (http://www.knight.org/advent/summa/summa.htm).

29. The Islamic concept of God does not consider attributes of loving and caring as essential to God's nature; see Norman L. Geisler and Abdul Saleeb, *Answering Islam: The Crescent in Light of the Cross* (Grand Rapids: Baker, 1993), pp. 133–137.

30. Lang, *Angels,* p. 43.

31. Lockyer, *Angels,* p. 83.

32. Lang, *Angels,* p. 88.

33. David O. Dykes, *Do Angels Really Exist? Separating Fact from Fantasy* (Lafayette, La.: Huntington House, 1996), p. 145.

34. Lockyer, *Angels,* p. 75.

35. Gary Kinnaman, *Angels Dark and Light* (Ann Arbor, Mich.: Servant, 1994), p. 66.

36. For such a work see philosopher Mortimer J. Adler's *The Angels and Us* (Collier Books–Macmillan, 1982).

37. For readers desiring more thorough studies of this issue, I would recommend the following books: *A General Introduction to the Bible, Revised and Expanded* by Norman L. Geisler and William E. Nix (Moody, 1986); *The New Testament Documents: Are They Reliable?* by F. F. Bruce (InterVarsity, 1943, rev. ed. 1960); *Evidence that Demands a Verdict* by Josh McDowell (Campus Crusade for Christ, 1972); and *Biblical Inspiration* by I. Howard Marshall (Eerdmans, 1982).

38. Norman L. Geisler and William E. Nix, *A General Introduction to the Bible* (Chicago: Moody, 1968), p. 241.

39. F. F. Bruce quoted in Josh McDowell, *Evidence that Demands a Verdict* (San Bernardino, Calif.: Campus Crusade for Christ, 1972), p. 58.

40. Geisler and Nix, *General Introduction*, p. 263.

41. See F. F. Bruce, *The New Testament Documents: Are They Reliable?* (Inter-Varsity, 1943, rev. ed. 1960) and John A. T. Robinson, *Can We Trust the New Testament?* (Grand Rapids: Eerdmans, 1977).

42. J. Harold Greenlee quoted in McDowell, *Evidence*, p. 53.

43. Ibid., p. 54.

44. Geisler and Saleeb, *Islam*, pp. 233–234.

45. John Warwick Montgomery quoted in McDowell, *Evidence*, p. 47.

46. Geisler and Saleeb, *Islam*, p. 233.

47. Peter W. Stoner, *Science Speaks*, 3rd rev. ed., 1969 (Chicago: Moody, 1958), p. 95.

48. Ibid., p. 107.

49. John Ankerberg, John Weldon and Walter C. Kaiser Jr., *The Case for Jesus the Messiah* (Eugene, Ore.: Harvest House, 1989), p. 21.

50. Colin Chapman, *The Case for Christianity*, 1983 ed. (Grand Rapids: Eerdmans, 1981), p. 231.

51. Josh McDowell and Bill Wilson, *He Walked among Us* (San Bernardino, Calif.: Here's Life, 1988), p. 119.

52. The common use of the word *soul* today includes what some distinguish as the *spirit*. For that reason I use the terms interchangeably.

53. *The Confessions of Saint Augustine*, trans. by Edward B. Pusey (New York: Modern Library, 1949), p. 3.

54. The apostle Paul expressed it like this: "Do you not know that the wicked will not inherit the kingdom of God? Do not be deceived: Neither the sexually immoral nor idolaters nor adulterers nor male prostitutes nor homosexual offenders nor thieves nor the greedy nor drunkards nor slanderers nor swindlers will inherit the kingdom of God. *And that is what some of you were.* But you were washed, you were sanctified, you were justified in the name of the Lord Jesus Christ and by the Spirit of our God" (1 Corinthians 6:9–11, emphasis added).

55. Simone Weil, *Gateway to God*, ed. by David Raper, 1974 ed. (Glasgow: Fontana Books/William Collins Sons, 1952), pp. 44–45.

Selected List
of Works Consulted

Adler, Mortimer J. *The Angels and Us.* New York: Collier Books–Macmillan, 1982.

Ankerberg, John and John Weldon. *The Facts on Angels.* Eugene, Ore.: Harvest House, 1995.

Ankerberg, John, John Weldon and Walter C. Kaiser Jr. *The Case for Jesus the Messiah.* Eugene, Ore.: Harvest House, 1989.

Aquinas, St. Thomas. *Summa Theologica.* Part I, Questions 50–64. Fathers of the English Dominican Province, trans. <http://www.knight.org/advent/summa/summa.htm>.

Barth, Karl. *Church Dogmatics: The Doctrine of Creation.* Vol. 3, Pt. 3. G. W. Bromiley and R. J. Ehrlich, trans. Edinburgh: T & T Clark, 1960.

Bowman, Robert M. Jr. "Angelmania: Sense and Nonsense about Angels" (course notebook). Atlanta: Atlanta Christian Apologetics Project, 1995.

Briscoe, Stuart. *The Apostles' Creed: Beliefs that Matter.* Wheaton, Ill.: Harold Shaw, 1994.

Bruce, F. F. *The New Testament Documents: Are They Reliable?* Rev. ed. 1960. Downers Grove, Ill.: InterVarsity, 1943.

Chapman, Colin. *The Case for Christianity.* 1983 ed. Grand Rapids: Eerdmans, 1981.

Calvin, John. *Institutes of the Christian Religion.* Ford Lewis Battles, trans. John T. McNeill, ed. Philadelphia: Westminster, 1960.

Connelly, Douglas. *Angels around Us.* Downers Grove, Ill.: InterVarsity, 1994.

Dake, Finis. *Heavenly Hosts: A Biblical Study of Angels.* Lawrenceville, Ga.: Dake, 1995.

Dickason, C. Fred. *Angels, Elect and Evil.* Chicago: Moody, 1975.

Dowley, Tim, ed. *Eerdmans' Handbook to the History of Christianity.* Guideposts ed. Grand Rapids: Eerdmans, 1977.

Dykes, David O. *Do Angels Really Exist? Separating Fact from Fantasy*. Lafayette, La.: Huntington House, 1996.

Gaebelein, A. C. *What the Bible Says about Angels*. Grand Rapids: Baker, 1987.

Garrett, Duane A. *Angels and the New Spirituality*. Nashville: Broadman & Holman, 1995.

Geisler, Norman L. and William E. Nix. *A General Introduction to the Bible*. Chicago: Moody, 1968.

Geisler, Norman L. and Abdul Saleeb. *Answering Islam: The Crescent in Light of the Cross*. Grand Rapids: Baker, 1993.

Graham, Billy. *Angels: God's Secret Agents*. 2nd ed. Dallas: Word, 1975.

Grudem, Wayne. *Systematic Theology: An Introduction to Biblical Doctrine*. Grand Rapids: Zondervan, 1994.

Jeremiah, David. *What the Bible Says about Angels: Powerful Guardians, a Mysterious Presence, God's Messengers*. Sisters, Ore.: Multnomah, 1996.

Jones, Timothy. *Celebration of Angels*. Nashville: Thomas Nelson, 1994.

Kittel, Gerhard. "Angelos, Archangelos, Isangelos." *Theological Dictionary of the New Testament*. Vol. 1. Gerhard Kittel, ed. Geoffrey W. Bromiley, trans. Grand Rapids: Eerdmans, 1968.

Kinnaman, Gary. *Angels Dark and Light*. Ann Arbor, Mich.: Servant, 1994.

Lang, Judith. *The Angels of God: Understanding the Bible*. London: New City Press, 1997.

Law, Terry. *The Truth About Angels*. Lake Mary, Fla.: Creation House, 1994.

Lockyer, Herbert. *All the Angels in the Bible*. Peabody, Mass.: Hendrickson, 1995.

Marshall, I. Howard. *Biblical Inspiration*. Grand Rapids: Eerdmans, 1982.

Marty, Martin E. *A Short History of Christianity*. Cleveland and New York: Fontana Books/William Collins + World, 1959.

McDowell, Josh. *Evidence that Demands a Verdict*. San Bernardino, Calif.: Campus Crusade for Christ, 1972.

McDowell, Josh and Bill Wilson. *He Walked among Us*. San Bernardino, Calif.: Here's Life, 1988.

Mounce, Robert H. "The Book of Revelation." *The New International Commentary on the New Testament*. Grand Rapids: Eerdmans, 1977.

Myers, Edward P. *A Study of Angels*. Rev. ed. 1994. West Monroe, La.: Howard, 1978.

Philip, George M. *The Apostles' Creed*. Scotland: Christian Focus, 1990.

Rhodes, Ron. *Angels among Us*. Eugene, Ore.: Harvest House, 1994.

Robinson, John A. T. *Can We Trust the New Testament?* Grand Rapids: Eerdmans, 1977.

Rosen, Moishe. *Y'shua*. Chicago: Moody, 1982.

Sire, James W. *Why Should Anyone Believe Anything at All?* Downers Grove, Ill.: InterVarsity, 1994.

Stoner, Peter W. *Science Speaks*. 3rd rev. ed. 1969. Chicago: Moody, 1958.

Weil, Simone. *Gateway to God*. David Raper, ed. 1974 ed. Glasgow: Fontana Books/William Collins, 1952.

Williams, J. Rodman. "Angels on Assignment." An unpublished paper. Anaheim, Calif.: Melodyland School of Theology, n.d. [1970s].

———. *Renewal Theology: God, the World and Redemption*. Grand Rapids: Zondervan, 1988.

Scripture Index

Robert W. Graves is the author of *Praying in the Spirit* and *Increasing Your Theological Vocabulary*. He is deputy land administrator of Fulton County, Atlanta, Georgia, and Christian education director at Roswell Assembly of God Church. Graves is a former adjunct professor in English at Georgia State University and a former faculty member at Southwestern Assemblies of God College (Waxahachie, Tex.). He and his wife, Debbie, have three children, Michael, Jonathan, and Maresha, and live in Woodstock, Georgia.